THE

LIFE

OF

REV. RICHARD BAXTER.

CHIEFLY COMPILED FROM HIS OWN WRITINGS.

PUBLISHED BY THE
AMERICAN TRACT SOCIETY,
150 NASSAU-STREET NEW YORK.

CONTENTS.

NOTE.

The life of this eminent servant of God, abounding with striking incidents, and adapted to be useful to all, is published nearly in the present form by the Religious Tract Society in London. Some corrections of obscure phraseology and antique style are here made, without altering the character of the narrative. The reader will be struck with his extraordinary reliance on the efficacy of prayer; his abundant labors as a pastor; the rudeness, ignorance, and persecuting spirit of the age in which he lived; his burning zeal for the spread of the Gospel at that early period of modern missions; the great variety of works he was enabled to write, though in a very low state of health; and the wonderful extent to which the powers of the mind may be kept up by the habitual exercise of them, even amid the multiplied infirmities of old age.

A more full account of the man, comprising a description of his voluminous writings, may be found by the student in "Baxter's Life and Times, by Rev. William Orme." 2 vols. octavo.

LIFE OF

THE

REV. RICHARD BAXTER.

CHAPTER I.

HIS EARLY LIFE AND CONVERSION.

RICHARD BAXTER was born at Rowton, Shropshire, (England,) on the 12th of November, 1615. He resided in that village with his maternal grandfather till he was nearly ten years of age, when he was taken home to live with his parents at Eaton Constantine, in the same county. His father, he says, "had the competent estate of a freeholder, free from the temptations of poverty and riches; but having been addicted to gaming in his youth, as was also his father before him, it was so entangled by debts, that it occasioned some excess of worldly cares before it was freed."

The father of Richard Baxter, about the time of his son's birth, became seriously impressed with the importance of divine truth, and appears to have subsequently become a sincere follower of the Redeemer. His conversion was effected chiefly through the instrumentality of reading the Scriptures. He had but few opportunities of attending on other means of grace. Many of the pulpits were occupied by ministers ignorant of the truth as it is in Jesus; and those who preached the Gospel in its purity were, for the most part, so despised and contemned, that it required no small share of moral courage to attend on their ministry. Converted himself, he became anxious for the salvation of his only son. He directed the attention of his youthful charge to the sacred Scriptures, whence he had himself derived so much benefit. Nor were his instructions and efforts altogether vain. Baxter thus ingenuously confesses his early sins and convictions, in his history of his own life and times:

"At first my father set me to read the historical parts of Scripture, which, suiting with my nature, greatly delighted me; and though all that time I neither understood nor relished much the doctrinal part and mystery of redemption, yet it did me good, by acquainting me with the matters of fact, and drawing me on to love the Bible, and to search by degrees into the rest.

"But though my conscience would trouble me when I sinned, yet divers sins I was addicted to, and often committed against my conscience; which, for the warning of others, I will here confess, to my shame.

"1. I was much addicted, when I feared correction, to lie, that I might escape.

"2. I was much addicted to the excessive gluttonous eating of apples and pears, which, I think, laid the foundation of that weakness of my stomach which caused the bodily calamities of my life.

"3. To this end, and to concur with naughty boys that gloried in evil, I have often gone into other men's orchards, and stolen their fruit, when I had enough at home.

"4. I was somewhat excessively addicted to play, and that with covetousness for money.

"5. I was extremely bewitched with a love of romances, fables, and old tales, which corrupted my affections and wasted my time.

"6. I was guilty of much idle foolish chat, and imitation of boys in scurrilous foolish words and actions, though I durst not swear.

"7. I was too proud of the commendations of my instructors, who all of them fed my pride, making me seven or eight years the highest in the school, and boasting of me to others; which, though it furthered my learning, yet helped not my humility.

"8. I was too bold and irreverent towards my parents.

"These were my sins, with which, in my childhood, conscience troubled me for a great while before they were overcome."

His convictions gathered strength, although occasionally resisted. The temptations to neglect religion were strong and powerful. The reproach cast on his father and others, who, for their desire and pursuit of holiness, were contemptuously designated "Puritans," proved for a season a stumbling-block in his path. Still, however, the reflecting mind of the son led him to discern the difference between the conduct of his father and that of his calumniators, and to conclude that there was more of reason and truth in a life of holiness, than in a life of impiety and rebellion against the majesty of heaven. He says:

"In the village where I lived, the Reader read the common prayer briefly; and the rest of the day, even till dark night almost, except eating time, was spent in dancing under a may-pole and a great tree, not far from my father's door, where all the town met together: and though one of my father's own tenants was the piper, he could not restrain him nor break the sport; so that we could not read the Scripture in our family without the great disturbance of the taber and pipe, and noise in the street!* Many times my mind was inclined to be among them, and sometimes I broke loose from my conscience and joined with them; and the more I did it, the more I was inclined to it. But when I heard them call my father 'Puritan,' it did much to cure me and alienate me from them; for I considered that my father's exercise of reading the Scripture was better than theirs, and would surely be judged better by all men at the last; and I considered what it was, for which he and others were thus derided. When I heard them speak scornfully of others, as Puritans, whom I never knew, I was at first apt to believe all the lies and slanders wherewith they loaded them; but when I heard my own father so reproached, and perceived that drunkards were the most forward in the reproach, I perceived that it was mere malice. For my father never objected to common prayer or ceremonies, nor spoke against bishops, nor ever so much as prayed but by a book or form, being unacquainted then with any that did otherwise. But only for reading Scripture when the rest were dancing on the Lord's day, and for praying by a form out of the end of the common prayer book, in his house, and for reproving drunkards and swearers, and for talking sometimes a few words of Scripture, and about the life to come, he was reviled commonly by the name of Puritan, Precisian and Hypocrite; and so were the godly ministers that lived in the country near us, not only by our neighbors, but by

* These profanations of the Lord's day were authorised and encouraged by the royal proclamation, called the Book of Sports, set forth A. D. 1618.—See Life of Bishop Hall, p. 36.

the common talk of the multitude all about us. By this observation I was fully convinced that godly people were the best; and those that despised them, and lived in sin and pleasure, were a malignant, unhappy sort of people; and this kept me out of their company, except now and then, when the love of sports and play enticed me."

When about fifteen years of age, "it pleased God," he writes, "of his wonderful mercy, to open my eyes with a clearer insight into the concerns and case of my own soul, and to touch my heart with a livelier feeling of things spiritual than ever I had found before." While under this concern, a poor man in the town lent his father an old torn book, entitled "Bunny's Resolutions." "In reading this book," he observes, "it pleased God to awaken my soul, and show me the folly of sinning, and the misery of the wicked, and the inexpressible weight of things eternal, and the necessity of resolving on a holy life, more than I was ever acquainted with before. The same things which I knew before, came now in another manner, with light, and sense, and seriousness to my heart."

"Yet, whether sincere conversion began now, or before, or after, I was never able to this day to know; for I had before had some love to the things and people that were good, and a restraint from sins, except those forementioned; and so much from most of those, that I seldom committed them, and when I did, it was with great reluctance. And, both now and formerly, I knew that Christ was the only mediator by whom we must have pardon, justification and life; but I had little lively sense of the love of God in Christ to the world or me, or of my special need of him!"

"About this time it pleased God that a poor pedlar

came to the door with ballads and some good books, and my father bought of him Dr. Sibbs' 'Bruised Reed.' This also I read, and found it suited to my taste, and seasonably sent me; which opened more the love of God to me, and gave me a livelier apprehension of the mystery of redemption, and of my obligations to Jesus Christ."

"After this, we had a servant who had a little piece of Mr. Perkins' works, 'Of Repentance,' and the 'Art of living and dying well,' and the 'Government of the Tongue;' and the reading of that did further inform me, and confirm me. And thus, *without any means but books*, was God pleased to resolve me for himself."

Various are the means by which God awakens the soul to a sense of its danger, and leads it to the knowledge and enjoyment of himself. The pulpit and the school, conversation and reading, correspondence and advice, have been employed as instruments in the hands of the Eternal Spirit in effecting the conversion of souls. To preaching, as the express appointment of God, must be ascribed the highest place; but inferior only to it is the instrumentality of religious books. In places where the preaching of the Gospel is unknown or unattended, the distribution of such books is of the utmost importance. To such books Baxter was greatly indebted for his conversion: and having derived so much benefit from this means, he ever after employed it extensively among his friends, his flock, and all to whom his influence would reach. The facilities afforded, in the present day, for the dissemination of religious knowledge are truly astonishing; and among others, the efforts of Religious Tract Societies, with their millions of publications, should not be overlooked.

Many will arise in the last day, and acknowledge that their conversion was effected by means of these publications. Nor is it the least advantage of these institutions, that they afford an opportunity to persons in the humblest circumstances to be instrumental in doing good to their fellow-creatures. They can give a Tract, though they cannot deliver a discourse; they can send a Tract where they cannot visit in person; they can circulate books where they cannot engage in religious conversation. In the formation of Baxter's early religious opinions and character, we see the instrumentality of a laborer, a pedlar, and a servant employed. The sovereignty of God is clearly seen in the agents and means of salvation. "His wisdom is unsearchable, and his ways are past finding out." "To God, only wise, be all the glory."

Baxter's early education was greatly neglected. His professed teachers were either incompetent to their task, or suffered him to be occupied rather as he chose than according to any regular plan. Notwithstanding this neglect and irregularity, he made considerable progress. He rose superior to every difficulty, and in due time became qualified to enter the university. He was persuaded, however, not to enter college, but to pursue his studies under the direction of Mr. Wickstead, chaplain to the council at Ludlow Castle. Being his only pupil, it was expected that, through the undivided attention of his tutor, his proficiency would be greater than either at Cambridge or Oxford. The preceptor became much attached to the pupil; but being in earnest quest of place and preferment, he neglected his charge. He allowed him "books and time enough," but never seriously attempted to instruct and improve his mind. Nor was this the only disadvantage attending his residence at Ludlow, for he was thrown into gay and fashionable society, and was exposed to the various temptations incident to such a situation. His religious principles were in danger of being corrupted or destroyed by the practice of gambling; but he was enabled, by the grace of God, to escape the snare, and to resist all subsequent attempts to lead him astray. In this situation he formed an intimacy with a young man of professed piety, but who, at length, by the seductive influence of liquor, became an apostate. At this period, however, he instructed young Baxter " in the way of God more perfectly;" prayed with him, exhorted and encouraged him in his religious course, and thus became of essential service to his young friend. Baxter remained with his tutor about a year and a half, and then returned home. At the request of lord Newport, he took the charge of the grammar school at Wroxeter for a short time, as the master was in a dying state. On his death, Baxter left this charge, and pursued his studies and religious inquiries under the direction of the venerable Mr. Garbett, a minister of Wroxeter.

The health of Baxter was in a precarious state, and, in the prospect of eternity, he became more solicitous to improve his remaining days in the worship, and ways and service of God. He says:

"Being in expectation of death, by a violent cough, with spitting of blood, &c. of two years continuance, supposed to be a consumption, I was awakened to be more solicitous about my soul's everlasting state; and I came so short of that sense and seriousness which a matter of such infinite weight required, that I was many years in doubt of my sincerity, and thought I had no spiritual life at all. I wondered at the senseless hardness of my heart, that I could think and talk of sin and hell, and Christ and grace, of God and heaven with no more feeling. I cried from day to day to God for grace against this senseless deadness. I called myself the most hard-hearted sinner, that could feel nothing of all that I knew and talked of. I was not then sensible of the incomparable excellence of holy love and delight in God, nor much employed in thanksgiving and praise; but all my groans were for more contrition and a broken heart, and I prayed most for tears and tenderness.

"Thus was I long kept with the calls of approaching death at one ear, and the questionings of a doubtful conscience at the other; and since then I have found that this method of God's was very wise, and no other was so likely to have tended to my good. These benefits of it I sensibly perceived:

"1. It made me vile and loathsome to myself, and made pride one of the most hateful sins in the world to me. I thought of myself as I now think of a detestable sinner, and my enemy: that is, with a love of benevolence, wishing them well, but with little love of complacency at all; and the long continuance of it tended the more effectually to a habit.

"2. It much restrained me from that sportful levity and vanity to which my nature and youthfulness much inclined me, and caused me to meet temptations to sensuality with the greatest fear, and made them less effectual against me.

"3. It made the doctrine of redemption the more savory to me, and my thoughts of Christ more serious and clear. I remember, in the beginning, how beneficial to me were Mr. Perkins' short treatise of the 'Right Knowledge of Christ crucified,' and his 'Exposition of the Creed,' because they taught me how to live by faith on Christ.

"4. It made the world seem to me as a carcass that had neither life nor loveliness, and it destroyed that ambitious desire after literary fame which was the sin of my childhood. I had a desire before to have attained the highest academical degrees and reputation of learning, and to have chosen out my studies accordingly; but sickness, and solicitousness for my doubting soul, shamed away all these thoughts as fooleries and children's plays.

"5. It set me upon that method of my studies, of which, since then, I have found the benefit, though at the time I was not satisfied with myself. It caused me first to seek God's kingdom and his righteousness, and most to mind the one thing needful; and to determine first on my ultimate end, by which I was engaged to choose out and prosecute all other studies but as meant to that end. Therefore divinity not only shared with the rest of my studies, but always had the first and chief place. And it caused me to study a practical divinity first, in the most practical books, in a practical order; doing all purposely for the informing and reforming of my own soul."

"And as for those doubts of my own salvation, which exercised me many years, the chief causes of them were these:

"1. Because I could not distinctly trace the workings of the Spirit upon my heart, in that method which Mr. Bolton, Mr. Hooker, Mr. Rogers, and other divines describe; nor knew the time of my conversion, being wrought on by the forementioned degrees. But, since then, I understood that the soul is in too dark and passionate a plight at first to be able to keep an exact account of the order of its own operations; and that preparatory grace, being sometimes longer and sometimes shorter, and the first degree of special grace being usually very small, it is not to be expected that many will be able to give a true account of the time when special grace began.

"2. My second doubt was as aforesaid, because of the hardness of my heart, or want of such lively apprehensions of things spiritual as I had about things corporeal. And though I still groan under this as my sin and want, yet I now perceive that a soul in flesh works so much after the manner of the flesh, that it much desires sensible apprehensions; but things spiritual and distant are not so apt to excite emotion and stir the passions.

"3. My next doubt was lest education and fear had done all that ever was done upon my soul, and regeneration and love were yet to be sought; because I had found conviction from my childhood, and found more fear than love in all my duties and restraints.

"But I afterwards perceived that education is an ordinary way for the conveyance of God's grace, and ought no more to be set in opposition to the Spirit, than the preaching of the word; and that it was the great mercy of God to begin with me so soon, and to prevent such sins as else might have been my shame and sorrow while I lived. And I understood, that, though fear without love be not a state of saving grace, and greater love to the world than to God be not consistent with sincerity, yet a little predominant love, prevailing against worldly love, conjoined with a far greater measure of fear, may be a state of special grace. And I found that my hearty love of the word of God, and of the servants of God, and my desires to be more holy, and especially the hatred of my heart for loving God no more, and my wish to love him, and be pleasing to him, were not without some true love to himself, though it appeared more sensibly afterwards.

"4. Another of my doubts was, because my grief and humiliation were no greater, and because I could weep no more for this.

"But I understood, at last, that God breaks not all men's hearts alike, and that the gradual proceedings of his grace might be one cause, and my nature, not apt to weep for other things, another; and that the change of our heart from sin to God is true repentance; and a loathing of ourselves is true humiliation; and that he that had rather leave his sin, than have leave to keep it, and had rather be the most holy, than have leave to be unholy or less holy, is neither without true repentance nor the love of God.

"5. Another of my doubts was, because I had, after my change, committed some sins deliberately and knowingly. And, be they ever so small, I thought, he that could sin upon knowledge and deliberation, had no true grace; and that, if I had but had as strong temptations to fornication, drunkenness, fraud, or other more heinous sins, I might also have committed them. And if these proved that I had then no saving grace, after all that I had felt, I thought it unlikely that ever I should have any."

"The means by which God was pleased to give me some peace and comfort were—

"1. The reading of many consolatory books.

"2. The observation of the condition of other men. When I heard many make the very same complaints that I did, who were people of whom I had the best esteem for the uprightness and holiness of their lives.

it much abated my fears and troubles. And, in particular, it much comforted me to read him whom I loved as one of the holiest of all the martyrs, John Bradford, subscribing himself so often, 'The hard-hearted sinner,' and 'The miserable hard-hearted sinner,' even as I was used to do myself.

"3. And it much increased my peace, when God's providence called me to the comforting of many others that had the same complaints. While I answered their doubts, I answered my own; and the charity which I was constrained to exercise for them, redounded to myself, and insensibly abated my fears, and procured me an increase of quietness of mind.

"And yet, after all, I was glad of probabilities instead of full undoubted certainties; and to this very day, though I have no such degree of doubtfulness as is any great trouble to my soul, or procures any great disquieting fears, yet I cannot say that I have such a certainty of my own sincerity in grace, as excludes all doubts and fears of the contrary."

Baxter's old preceptor induced him for a season to lay aside all thoughts of the ministry, and to become an attendant at court. He resided for a month at Whitehall, but became so disgusted with the scenes and practices of high life, that his conscience would not allow his longer continuance from home. He says: "I had, quickly, enough of the court; when I saw a stage-play, instead of a sermon, on the Lord's day in the afternoon, and saw what course was there in fashion, and heard little preaching but what was, in some part, against the puritans, I was glad to be gone. At the same time, it pleased God, my mother fell sick, and desired my return; and so I resolved to bid farewell to those kinds of employments and expectations."

When he was going home into the country, about Christmas day, A. D. 1634, he relates that, on meeting a loaded wagon, his horse fell on the side of a bank, by which he was thrown before the wheel, which he says "had gone over me, but that, as it pleased God, the horses suddenly stopped, without any discernable cause, till I was recovered; which commanded me to observe the mercy of my Protector."

On his return he found his mother extremely ill. She lingered till May, and then expired.

Baxter's own health was in a very precarious state; but he was anxiously desirous of doing good during the short time which he supposed would be allotted to him on earth. He states:

"My own soul being under serious apprehensions of another world, I was exceedingly desirous to communicate those apprehensions to ignorant, presumptuous, careless sinners. But I was in a very great perplexity between my encouragements and my discouragements. I was conscious of my personal insufficiency, for want of that measure of learning and experience which so great and high a work required. I knew that the want of academical honors and degrees was likely to make me contemptible with the most, and consequently hinder the success of my endeavors. But yet, expecting to be so quickly in another world, the great concerns of miserable souls prevailed with me against all these impediments; and being conscious of a thirsty desire of men's conversion and salvation, and of some competent persuading faculty of expression which fervent affections might help to actuate, I resolved, that if one or two souls only might be won to God, it would recompense all the dishonor I might receive from men!"

CHAPTER II.

HIS ORDINATION, AND FIRST PUBLIC ENGAGEMENTS.

Baxter was induced, by the advice of his friend Berry, to accept the head mastership of a newly endowed grammar school at Dudley, Worcestershire. He was the more ready to accept this situation, as it would afford him an opportunity of preaching in that unenlightened neighborhood. He applied for ordination to the Bishop of Winchester, which, after examination and subscription, was duly administered. He, moreover, received the bishop's license to teach in the school at Dudley. In a subsequent period of his life, he dedicated his treatise on "Self-denial" to his friend Colonel Berry, whose character had undergone a considerable change. The following passage from his dedicatory letter describes his views and feelings on entering the ministry, and his obligation to his friend and adviser. "You brought me into the ministry. I am confident you know to what ends, and with what intentions I desired it. I was then very ignorant, young, and raw. Though my weakness be yet such as I must lament, I must say, to the praise of the great Shepherd of the flock, that he hath, since then, afforded me precious opportunities, much assistance, and as much encouragement as to any man that I know alive. You know my education and initial weakness were such as forbid me to glory in the flesh; but I will not rob God of his glory to avoid the appearance of ostentation, lest I be proud of seeming not to be proud. I doubt not but many thousand souls will thank you, when they have read that you were the man that led me into the ministry."

"Being settled in the new school at Dudley, I there preached my first public sermon in the upper parish church, and afterwards preached in the villages about; and there had occasion to enter afresh upon the study of *Conformity*;* for there were many private Christians thereabouts that were non-conformists, and one in the house with me. And that excellent man, Mr. William Fenner, had lately lived two miles off, at Sedgley, who, by defending conformity, and honoring it by a wonderfully powerful and successful way of preaching, conference, and holy living, had stirred up the non-conformists the more to a vehement pleading of their cause. And though they were there generally godly honest people, yet they were smartly censorious, and made conformity no small fault. And they lent me manuscripts and books which I never saw before; whereupon I thought it my duty to set upon a serious impartial trial of the whole cause.

"In the town of Dudley I lived in much comfort, amongst a poor tractable people, lately noted for drunkenness, but commonly more ready to hear God's word with submission and reformation than most places where I have been, so that having, since the wars, set up a monthly lecture there, the church was usually as much crowded within, and at the windows, as ever I saw any London congregation; partly through the great willingness of the people, and partly by the exceeding populousness of the country, where the woods and commons are planted with nailers, scythe-smiths, and other iron laborers, like a continued village.

* To the enactments of the established church.

"When I had been but three quarters of a year at Dudley, I was, by God's very gracious providence, invited to Bridgnorth, the second town of Shropshire, to preach there, as assistant to the worthy pastor of that place. As soon as I heard the place described, I judged it was the fittest for me; for there was just such employment as I desired and could submit to without violating conscience, and some probability of peace and quietness.

"But the people proved a very ignorant, dead-hearted people, the town consisting too much of inns and ale-houses, and having no general trade to employ the inhabitants, which is the undoing of many large towns. So that though, through the great mercy of God, my first labors were not without success in the conversion of some ignorant and careless sinners to him, and were over-valued by those that were already regardful of the concerns of their souls, yet they were not so successful as they proved afterwards in other places. Though I was in the fervor of my affections, and never any where preached with more vehement desires of men's conversion, yet, with the generality, applause of the preacher was most of the success of the sermon which I could hear of; and their tippling, and ill-company, and dead-heartedness quickly drowned all."

Though a friend to episcopacy, yet the omission of some required ceremonies, together with his refusal to take the "et cetera" oath, (binding him never to give his consent to alter the government of the church in particulars not distinctly defined,) had nearly occasioned his expulsion from the ministry, and the loss of his liberty, if not, in his weak and infirm state of health, of life itself. Indeed, some of his accusers threatened him with "hanging" if he did not comply. God, however, in whose hands are the hearts of all men, changed the purposes and restrained the malice of his adversaries. He continued to preach at Bridgnorth a year and three-quarters, in the uninterrupted enjoyment of liberty, which, says he, " I took to be a very great mercy to me in these troublesome times."

He says, " The long parliament, among other parts of their reformation, resolved to reform the corrupted clergy, and appointed a committee to receive petitions and complaints against them; which was no sooner understood, but multitudes in all countries came up with petitions against their ministers."

" Among all these complainers, the town of Kidderminister, in Worcestershire, drew up a petition against their minister. The vicar of the place they represented as utterly insufficient for the ministry; presented by a papist; unlearned; preaching but once a quarter, and that so feebly as exposed him to laughter, and showed that he understood not the essential articles of Christianity; as one that frequented ale houses; had sometimes been drunk, &c.

" The vicar, knowing his insufficiency, and hearing how two others in this case had fared, desired to compound the business with them, which was soon accomplished. Hereupon they invited me to them from Bridgnorth. The bailiff of the town, and all the feoffees, desired me to preach with them, in order to a full determination. My mind was much to the place, as soon as it was described to me, because it was a full congregation, with a most convenient temple; they were an ignorant, rude and revelling people for the most part, who had need of preaching; and yet had among them a small company of converts, humble, godly and of good conversation, and not much hated by the rest, and therefore the fitter to assist their teacher: but above all, because they had hardly ever had any lively, serious preaching among them. For Bridgnorth had made me resolve that I would never more go among a people that had been hardened in unprofitableness under an awakening ministry; but either to such as never had any convincing preacher, or to such as had profited by him. As soon as I came to Kidderminster, and had preached there one day, I was chosen, without opposition; for though fourteen only had the power of choosing, they desired to please the rest. And thus I was brought, by the gracious providence of God, to that place which had the chief of my labors, and yielded me the greatest fruits. And I noted the mercy of God in this, that I never went to any place in my life, among all my changes, which I had before designed, or thought of, much less sought, but only to those that I never thought of, till the sudden invitation surprised me."

CHAPTER III.

HIS LABORS, TRIALS, AND SUCCESS AT KIDDERMINSTER.

To this important and interesting scene of labor Baxter was invited on the 9th of March, 1640. His legal appointment, after laboring among the people during the interval, is dated April 5, 1641.

For this station of public and extensive usefulness, he had been prepared by various painful and alarming afflictions. He says: " All this forementioned time of my ministry was passed under my foredescribed weaknesses, which were so great as made me live and preach in continual expectation of death, supposing still that I had not long to live. And this I found, through all my life, to be an invaluable mercy to me: for—

"1. It greatly weakened temptations.

"2. It kept me in great contempt of the world.

"3. It taught me highly to esteem time; so that, if any of it passed away in idleness or unprofitableness, it was so long a pain and burden to my mind. So that I must say, to the praise of my most wise Conductor, that time has still seemed to me much more precious than gold, or any earthly gain, and its minutes have not been despised, nor have I been much tempted to any of the sins which go under the name of pastime, since I undertook my work.

"4. It made me study and preach things necessary, and a little stirred up my sluggish heart to speak to sinners with some compassion, as a dying man to dying men.

"These, with the rest which I mentioned before, when I spake of my infirmities, were the benefits which God afforded me by affliction. I humbly bless his gracious providence, who gave me his treasure in an earthen vessel, and trained me up in the school of affliction, and taught me the cross of Christ so soon, that I might be rather, as Luther speaks, 'a cross-bearer, than a cross-maker, or imposer.'"

His spiritual conflicts, too, were of a distressing character, and tended, eventually, by the grace of God, to qualify him to be an instructor of others, both as a preacher and writer. He says:

"At one time, above all the rest, struggling under a new and unusual disease, which put me upon the present expectation of my change, and *going for comfort* to the promises, as I was used, the tempter strongly assaulted my faith, and would have drawn me towards infidelity itself. Till I was ready to enter into the ministry, all my troubles had been raised by the hardness of my heart and the doubtings of my own sincerity; but now all these began to vanish, and never much returned to this day. And, instead of these, I was now assaulted with more pernicious temptations; especially to question the certain truth of the sacred Scriptures; and also the life to come, and the immortality of the soul. And these temptations assaulted me, not as they do the melancholy, with horrid vexing importunity; but, by pretence of sober reason, they would have drawn me to a settled doubting of Christianity.

"And here I found my own miscarriage and the great mercy of God. My miscarriage, in that I had so long neglected the well settling of the foundations on which I rested, while I had bestowed so much time in the superstructure and the applicatory part. For, not daring to question the truth of the Scriptures and the life to come, I had either taken it for a certainty upon trust, or taken up with common reasons of it, which I had never well considered, digested, or made my own; insomuch, that when this temptation came, it seemed at first to answer and enervate all the former reasons of my feeble faith, which made me take the Scriptures for the word of God; and it set before me such mountains of difficulty in the incarnation, the person of Christ, his undertaking and performance, with the scripture chronology, histories, style, &c. as had overwhelmed me, if God had not been my strength. And here I saw much of the mercy of God, that he let not out these terrible and dangerous temptations upon me while I was weak and in the infancy of my faith; for then I had never been able to withstand them. But faith is like a tree whose top is small while the root is young and shallow; and therefore, as then it has but small rooting, so it is not liable to the shaking winds and tempests as the large and high-grown trees are; but, as the top rises higher, so the root at once grows greater and deeper fixed, to cause it to endure its greater assaults.

"Though formerly I was wont, when any such temptation came, to cast it aside, as fitter to be abhorred than considered, yet now this would not give me satisfaction; but I was disposed to dig to the very foundations, and seriously to examine the reasons of Christianity, and to give a hearing to all that could be said against it, that so my faith might be indeed my own. And at last I found that 'Nothing is so firmly believed as that which has been some time doubted.'

"In the storm of this temptation, I questioned awhile whether I were indeed a Christian or an infidel, and whether faith could consist with such doubts as I was conscious of. For I had read, in the works of papists and protestants, that faith had certainty, and was more than an opinion; and that, if a man should live a godly life, from the bare apprehensions of the probability of the truth of Scripture and the life to come, it would not save him, as being no true godliness or faith. But my judgment closed with the reason of Dr. Jackson's determination of this case, which supported me much; that as in the very assenting act of faith there may be such weakness as may make us cry—'Lord, increase our faith: we believe; Lord, help our belief;' so, when faith and unbelief are in their conflict, it is the effects which must show us which of them is victorious. And that he that has so much faith as will cause him to deny himself, take up his cross, and forsake all the profits, honors, and pleasures of this world, for the sake of Christ, the love of God, and the hope of glory, has a saving faith, how weak soever. For God cannot condemn the soul that truly loves and seeks him ; and those that Christ brings to persevere in the love of God, he brings to salvation. And there were divers things that, in this assault, proved great assistances to my faith."

"From this assault I was forced to take notice that our belief of the truth of the word of God, and the life to come, is the spring of all grace; and with which it rises or falls, flourishes or decays, is actuated or stands still: and that there is more of this secret unbelief at the root than most of us are aware of; and that our love of the world, our boldness in sin, our neglect of duty, are caused hence. I observed easily in myself, that if at any time Satan, more than at other times, weakened my belief of Scripture and the life to come, my zeal in every religious duty abated with it, and I grew more indifferent in religion than before. I was more inclined to conformity in those points which I had taken to be sinful, and was ready to think, Why should I be singular, and offend the bishops and other superiors, and make myself contemptible in the world, and expose myself to censures, scorns and sufferings, and all for such little things as these, when the foundations themselves have such great difficulties as I am unable to overcome? But when faith revived, then none of the parts or concerns of religion seemed small; and then man seemed nothing, and the world a shadow and God was all.

"In the beginning, I doubted not of the truth of the

Holy Scriptures, or of the life to come, because I saw not the difficulties which might cause doubting. After that, I saw them, and I doubted, because I saw not that which should satisfy the mind against them. Since that, having seen both difficulties and evidences, though I am not so unmolested as at the first, yet is my faith, I hope, much stronger, and far better able to repel the temptations of Satan, and the sophisms of infidels, than before. But yet it is my daily prayer that God would increase my faith, and give my soul a clear sight of the evidences of his truth, and of himself, and of the invisible world."

Nor was Baxter exempt from slander: his moral character was assailed by base and unfounded calumnies. These he was enabled successfully to refute. His chief calumniator was obliged to confess that the charges were fabrications, and to beg his forgiveness, which was freely given.

The trials of ministers are frequently of a painful character, but, like those of private Christians, "they work together for good." They are over-ruled, not only for their personal benefit, but for the edification of their flocks. "If their sufferings abound, so do their consolations also," and that in order to their being the comforters of others. 2 Cor. 1 : 1–5.

Baxter entered on his work with spirit and zeal; nor was he suffered to labor long without witnessing blessed results in the conversion of sinners to God. At first he used to register the names, characters, &c. of his converts; but they became, at length, so numerous, that he discontinued the practice.

He continued successfully discharging his ministerial and pastoral labors for nearly two years, when the civil wars (growing out of a rupture between the king and his parliament) threw the whole country into confusion. His situation, though he was no partizan, was critical and dangerous. He was at length advised by his friends to retire from Kidderminster till public affairs should assume a more peaceable aspect. The immediate occasion of his leaving, he thus describes:

"About that time the parliament sent down an order for the demolishing of all statues and images of any of the three persons in the blessed Trinity, or of the virgin Mary, which should be found in churches, or on the crosses in churchyards. My judgment was for the obeying of this order, thinking it came from just authority; but I meddled not in it, but left the churchwarden to do what he thought good. The churchwarden, an honest, sober, quiet man, seeing a crucifix upon the cross in the churchyard, set up a ladder to have reached it, but it proved too short: whilst he was gone to seek another, a crew of the drunken riotous party of the town, poor journeymen and servants, took the alarm, and ran together with weapons to defend the crucifix and the church images, of which there were many remaining since the time of popery. The report was among them that I was the actor, and it was me they sought; but I was walking almost a mile out of town, or else, I suppose, I had there ended my days. When they missed me and the churchwarden both, they went raving about the streets to seek us. Two neighbors that dwelt in other parishes, hearing that they sought my life, ran in among them to see whether I were there, and they knocked them both down in the streets; and both of them are since dead, and, I think, never perfectly recovered of the wounds then received. When they had foamed about half an hour, and met with none of us, I came in from my walk, and hearing the people cursing at me in their doors, I wondered what the matter was, but quickly found how fairly I had escaped. The next Lord's day I dealt plainly with them, and laid open to them the quality of that action, and told them, seeing they so requited me as to seek my blood, I was willing to leave them, and save them from that guilt. But the poor sots were so amazed and ashamed that they took on sorrily, and were reluctant to part with me.

"About this time the king's declarations were read in our market-place, and the Reader, a violent country gentleman, seeing me pass the streets, stopped, and said, 'There goes a traitor,' without ever giving a syllable of reason for it.

"And the commission of array was set afoot, for the parliament meddled not with the militia of that county, Lord Howard, their lieutenant, not appearing. Then the rage of the rioters grew greater than before. And in preparation for the war, they had got the word among them—'Down with the roundheads;' insomuch that if a stranger passed in many places, that had short hair and a civil habit, the rabble presently cried, 'Down with the roundheads;' and some they knocked down in the open streets.

"In this fury of the rabble I was advised to withdraw awhile from home; whereupon I went to Gloucester. As I passed but through a corner of the suburbs of Worcester, they that knew me not cried, 'Down with the roundheads;' and I was glad to spur on and begone. But when I came to Gloucester, among strangers also that had never known me, I found a civil, courteous, and religious people, as different from Worcester as if they had lived under another government."

"When I had been at Gloucester a month, my neighbors of Kidderminster came for me home, and told me that if I stayed any longer the people would interpret it either that I was afraid, upon some guilt, or that I was against the king; so I bid my host, Mr. Darney, the town-clerk, and my friends, farewell, and never went to Gloucester more.

"For myself, I knew not what course to take. To live at home I was uneasy; but especially now, when soldiers, on one side or other, would be frequently among us, and we must be still at the mercy of every furious beast that would make a prey of us. I had neither money nor friends. I knew not who would receive me in any place of safety; nor had I any thing to satisfy them for my diet and entertainment. Hereupon I was persuaded, by one that was with me, to go to Coventry, where one of my old acquaintance was minister, Mr. Simon King, some time schoolmaster at Bridgnorth. So thither I went, with a purpose to stay there till one side or other had got the victory, and the war was ended, and then to return home.

"Whilst I was thinking what course to take, the committee and governor of the city desired me that I would stay with them, and lodge in the governor's house, and preach to the soldiers. The offer suited well with my necessities, but I resolved that I would not be chaplain to the regiment, nor take a commission; but, if the mere preaching of a sermon once or twice a week to the garrison would satisfy them, I would accept of the offer, till I could go home again. Here I lived in the governor's house, and followed my studies as quietly as in a time of peace, for about a year. only preaching once a week to the soldiers, and once on the Lord's day to the people, not taking from any of them a penny for either, save my diet only."

The war continued with unabated fury and severity. During his stay at Coventry he was invited by Cromwell to become chaplain to his troops which lay at Cambridge. This invitation he declined; but some time after, on learning the state of the army and the prospects of usefulness among the soldiers, at the solicitation of Captain Evanson, he became chaplain to Colonel Whalley's regiment, and left his quarters at Coventry, to the deep and universal regret of the residents in the garrison.

On joining his regiment he writes:

"I set myself, from day to day, to find out the corruptions of the soldiers, and to adapt my discourses and conversation to their mistakes, both religious and political. My life among them was a daily contending against seducers, and gently arguing with the more tractable."

His "efforts to do good" were unremitting. His time was occupied "in preaching, conference, and disputing against confounding errors," and in directing and comforting believers under the difficulties and perils of the times. His success, however, did not equal his expectations: party spirit ran exceedingly high; the soldiers were divided in their religious opinions; the camp afforded but few facilities for collecting any considerable numbers together, and besides, was constantly changing its position, according to the direction of war. And probably his desire to reconcile their religious differences, and to unite them under one religious discipline, led him more frequently to dispute than to preach, to dwell more on the details and minutiæ of the Gospel than on its essential truths; to labor as though they were at peace and had time for punctilios, rather than as being in a state of war, and in danger every hour of being hurried into eternity. These, with other untoward circumstances, contributed to diminish the probability of success, but at the same time to illustrate the zeal, the piety, and the perseverance of the conscientious chaplain. He was never in any engagement, nor took part, personally, in any contests, though present at some sieges.

After the fatal battle of Worcester, with health enfeebled by his excessive exertions in the army, he visited his old flock at Kidderminster, and thence proceeded to London for medical advice. His physician directed him to visit Tunbridge Wells, and try the efficacy of its waters. With this advice he complied. His health was in consequence improved, and in due time he returned to his quarters in Worcestershire, where the army still lay.

In all his peregrinations with the army and otherwise, he preached in most of the churches in the towns through which he passed; and no doubt can be entertained that his earnest, affectionate, and faithful preaching was attended with important results.

While staying at the house of Sir John Cook, Melborne, Derbyshire, he was seized with a violent bleeding at the nose, which so reduced his strength that his case was considered almost hopeless. His countenance was so altered as scarcely to be recognized by his most intimate friends. As soon as he could remove, he visited a friend in Leicestershire, where he remained three weeks in an exhausted state. In this state he was invited by his friends Sir Thomas and Lady Rous to take lodgings at their mansion. Thither he was conveyed, and experienced the greatest kindness and attention. At the end of three months, having recovered his strength, he returned to Kidderminster.

During this period of sickness and retirement from public labors; he was anxious to be useful, and to be restored, if agreeable to the Divine will, that his usefulness might be increased. He states concerning himself, "Being conscious that my time had not been improved to the service of God as I wished it had been, I put up many an earnest prayer to God that he would restore me, and use me more successfully in his work. And, blessed be that mercy which heard my groans in the day of my distress, and granted my desires, and wrought my deliverance, when men and means failed, and gave me opportunity to celebrate his praise."

It was during this affliction that he wrote his celebrated work, "the Saints' Everlasting Rest:"* a work, the usefulness of which no mortal can estimate. It was a blessing to the age in which he lived, and will continue to be so to the remotest ages of time. Had he lived only to write this work, his name would have been held in "everlasting remembrance."

His own account of the origin and progress of the work is interesting. "The second book which I wrote, and the first which I began, was that called 'The Saints' Everlasting Rest.' Whilst I was in health, I had not the least thought of writing books, or of serving God in any more public way than preaching; but, when I was weakened with great bleeding, and left solitary in my chamber, at Sir John Cook's, in Derbyshire, without any acquaintance but my servant about me, and was sentenced to death by the physicians, I began to contemplate more seriously the everlasting rest which I apprehended myself to be just on the borders of. And that my thoughts might not too

* Published by the American Tract Society

much scatter in my meditation, I began to write something on that subject, intending but the quantity of a sermon or two, but being continued long in weakness, where I had no books, and no better employment, I pursued it, till it was enlarged to the bulk in which it is published. The first three weeks I spent in it was at Mr. Nowel's, in Leicestershire; a quarter of a year more, at the seasons which so great weakness would allow, I bestowed on it at the house of Sir Thomas Rous, in Worcestershire; and I finished it, shortly after, at Kidderminster. The first and last parts were first done, being all that I intended for my own use; and the second and third parts were written afterwards, beyond my first intention.

This book it pleased God so far to bless to the profit of many, that it encouraged me to be guilty of all those writings which afterwards followed. The marginal citations I put in after I came home to my books; but almost all the book itself was written when I had no book but a Bible and a concordance. And I found that the transcript of the heart has the greatest force on the hearts of others. For the good that I have heard that multitudes have received by that book, and the benefit which I have again received by their prayers, I here humbly return my thanks to Him that compelled me to write it."

Anticipating that some objection might be made in respect to its style, he says, in his dedication of the work to the people of Kidderminster, "It is no wonder, therefore, if I am too abrupt in the beginning, seeing I then intended but the length of a sermon or two. Much less may you wonder if the whole is very imperfect, seeing it was written, as it were, with one foot in the grave, by a man that was betwixt living and dead, that wanted strength of nature to quicken invention or affection, and had no book but his Bible until the chief part was finished, nor had any regard to human ornaments. But, O how sweet is this providence now to my review! that so happily forced me to the work of meditation, which I had formerly found so profitable to my soul! and showed me more mercy in depriving me of other helps than I was aware of! and has caused my thoughts to feed on this heavenly subject, which has more benefited me than all the studies of my life!"

On his recovery he received a pressing invitation to return to his old charge at Kidderminster, which he instantly and cordially accepted. He was devotedly attached to his people, and considered himself bound to resist all attempts to procure his services in other places. He thus affectionately writes to "his beloved friends:" "If either I or my labors have any public use or worth, it is wholly, though not only yours; and I am convinced, by providence, that it is the will of God it should be so. This I clearly discerned on my first coming to you, in my former abode with you, and in the time of my forced absence from you. When I was separated by the miseries of the late unhappy wars, I durst not fix in any other congregation, but lived in a military unpleasing state, lest I should forestall my return to you, for whom I conceived myself reserved. The offer of great worldly accommodations, with five times the means I receive with you, was no temptation to me once to question whether I should leave you. Your free invitation of my return, your obedience to my doctrine, the strong affection I have yet towards you, above all people, and the general hearty return of love which I find from you, do all persuade me that

I was sent into the world especially for the service of your souls."

He resumed his labors under great bodily weakness, "being seldom an hour free from pain." He was subject to repeated attacks, from which he recovered, according to his own account, chiefly through the intercessions and fervent prayers of his friends. "Many a time have I been brought very low, and received the sentence of death in myself, when my poor, honest, praying neighbors have met, and, upon their fasting and earnest prayers, I have recovered. Once, when I had continued very feeble three weeks, and was unable to go abroad, the very day that they prayed for me I recovered, and was able to preach on the following Sabbath, and administered the Lord's supper; and was better after it, it being the first time that ever I administered it. And ever after that, whatever weakness was upon me, when I had, after preaching, administered that ordinance to many hundred people, I was much revived and eased of my infirmities."

"O how often," he writes in his 'Dying Thoughts,' "have I cried to Him, when men and means were nothing, and when no help in second causes appeared; and how often, and suddenly, and mercifully has he delivered me! What sudden ease, what removal of long affliction have I had! Such extraordinary changes, beyond my own and others' expectations, when many plain-hearted, upright Christians have, by fasting and prayer, sought God on my behalf, as have over and over convinced me of a special providence, and that God is indeed a hearer of prayer. And wonders have I seen done for others also, upon such prayer, more than for myself: yea, and wonders for the church, and for public societies." "Shall I therefore forget how often he has heard prayers for me? and how wonderfully he often has helped both me and others; my faith has been helped by such experiences, and shall I forget them, or question them without cause at last?"

Baxter relates several extraordinary instances of answers to prayer, in the recovery and preservation both of himself and friends. He was attentive in seeking such blessings, and in observing such circumstances; and, as an old divine justly observes, "they that watch providence shall never want a providence to watch." Having now brought down Baxter's life to the period when he settled again amongst his old friends, and resumed his accustomed labors, it will be desirable to introduce, in an abridged form, his own account of his "employments, success, and advantages," during his fourteen years' continuance among them.

1. Employments.

"I preached, before the wars, twice each Lord's day; but, after the war, but once, and once every Thursday, besides occasional sermons. Every Thursday evening, my neighbors that were most desirous, and had opportunity, met at my house, and there one of them repeated the sermon; and afterwards they proposed what doubts any of them had about the sermon, or any other case of conscience, and I resolved their doubts. And, last of all, I caused sometimes one, and sometimes another of them to pray, sometimes praying with them myself. Once a week, also, some of the young who were not prepared to pray in so great an assembly, met among a few more privately, where they spent three hours in prayer together. Every Saturday night they met at some of their houses to repeat the sermon of the last Lord's day, and to pray and prepare themselves for the following day. Once in a few weeks we had a day of humiliation, on one occasion or other. Two days every week my assistant and myself took fourteen families between us for private catechising and conference; he going through the parish, and the town coming to me. I first heard them recite the words of the catechism, and then examined them about the sense, and lastly urged them, with all possible engaging reason and vehemence, to answerable affection and practice. If any of them were perplexed through ignorance or bashfulness, I forbore to press them any farther to answers, but made them hearers, and either examined others, or turned all into instruction and exhortation. But this, I have opened more fully in my 'Reformed Pastor.' I spent about an hour with a family, and admitted no others to be present, lest bashfulness should make it burdensome, or any should talk of the weaknesses of others. So that all the afternoons, on Mondays and Tuesdays, I spent in this, after I had begun it; for it was many years before I attempted it; and my assistant spent the mornings of the same days in the same employment. Before that, I only catechised them in the church, and conferred with, now and then one occasionally.

"Besides all this, I was forced five or six years, by the people's necessity, to practise physic. A common pleurisy happening one year, and no physician being near, I was forced to advise them, to save their lives; and I could not afterwards avoid the importunity of the town and country round about. And because I never once took a penny of any one, I was crowded with patients, so that almost twenty would be at my door at once; and though God, by more success than I expected, so long encouraged me, yet, at last, I could endure it no longer; partly because it hindered my other studies, and partly because the very fear of miscarrying and doing any one harm, made it an intolerable burden to me. So that, after some years' practice, I procured a godly diligent physician to come and live in town, and bound myself, by promise, to practise no more, unless in consultation with him in case of any seeming necessity. And so with that answer I turned them all off, and never meddled with it more."

2. Success.

"I have mentioned my sweet and acceptable employment; let me, to the praise of my gracious Lord, acquaint you with some of my success. And I will not suppress it, though I foreknow that the malignant will impute the mention of it to pride and ostentation. For it is the sacrifice of thanksgiving which I owe to my most gracious God, which I will not deny him for fear of being censured as proud, lest I prove myself proud indeed, while I cannot undergo the imputation of pride in the offering of my thanks for such undeserved mercies.

"My public preaching met with an attentive, diligent auditory. Having broke over the brunt of the opposition of the rabble before the wars, I found them afterwards tractable and unprejudiced.

"Before I ever entered into the ministry, God blessed my private conference to the conversion of some, who remain firm and eminent in holiness to this day. Then, and in the beginning of my ministry, I was wont to number them as jewels; but since then I could not keep any number of them.

"The congregation was usually full, so that we were led to build five galleries after my coming thither, the church itself being very capacious, and the most commodious and convenient that ever I was in.

Our private meetings also were full. On the Lord's day there was no disorder to be seen in the streets, but you might hear a hundred families singing psalms and repeating sermons, as you passed through the streets. In a word, when I came thither first, there was about one family in a street that worshipped God and called on his name; and when I came away, there were some streets where there was not more than one family in the side of a street that did not so; and that did not, in professing serious godliness, give us hopes of their sincerity. And of those families which were the worst, being inns and ale-houses, usually some persons in each house did seem to be religious. Though our administration of the Lord's supper was so ordered as displeased many, and the far greater part kept themselves away, yet we had six hundred that were communicants, of whom there were not twelve that I had not good hopes of, as to their sincerity; and those few that came to our communion, and yet lived scandalously, were excommunicated afterwards. And I hope there were many who feared God that came not to our communion, some of them being kept off by husbands, by parents, by masters, and some dissuaded by men that differed from us.

"When I commenced personal conference with each family and catechising them, there were very few families in all the town that refused to come; and those few were beggars at the town's ends, who were so ignorant that they were ashamed it should be manifest. And few families went from me without some tears, or seemingly serious promises for a godly life. Yet many ignorant and ungodly persons there were still among us; but most of them were in the parish, and not in the town, and in those parts of the parish which were farthest from the town. Some of the poor men competently understood the body of divinity, and were able to judge in difficult controversies. Some of them were so able in prayer, that very few ministers equalled them in order and fullness, apt expressions, holy oratory, and fervency. A great number of them were able to pray very appropriately with their families, or with others. The temper of their minds, and the correctness of their lives, were even more commendable than their talents. The professors of serious godliness were generally of very humble minds and conduct; of meek and quiet behavior towards others; and blameless in their conversation.

"And in my poor endeavors with my brethren in the ministry, my labors were not lost. Our discussions proved not unprofitable; our meetings were never contentious, but always comfortable. We took great delight in the company of each other; so that I know the remembrance of those days is pleasant both to them and me. When discouragements had long kept me from proposing a way of church order and discipline which all might agree in, that we might neither have churches ungoverned, nor fall into divisions among ourselves at the first mention of it, I found a readier consent than I could expect, and all went on without any great difficulties. And when I attempted to bring them all conjointly to the work of catechising and instructing every family by itself, I found a ready consent in most, and performance in many. So that I must here, to the praise of my dear Redeemer, set up this pillar of remembrance, even to his praise who hath employed me so many years in so comfortable a work, with such encouraging success! O what am I, a worthless worm, not only wanting academical honors, but much of that furniture which is needful to so high a work, that God should thus abundantly encourage me, when the reverend instructors of my youth labored fifty years together in one place, and could scarcely say they had been instrumental in the conversion of even one or two of their hearers. And the greater was this mercy, because I was naturally of a desponding spirit; so that if I had preached one year, and seen no fruits of it, I should hardly have forborne running away like Jonah, but should have thought that God called me not to that place."

3. Advantages.

"Having related my encouraging successes in this place, I shall next tell you by what and how many advantages so much was effected, under that grace which worketh by means, though with a free diversity; which I do for the help of others in managing ignorant and sinful people.

"One advantage was, that I came to a people that never had any awakening ministry before. For if they had been hardened under a powerful ministry, and been sermon proof, I should have expected less.

"Another advantage was, that at first I was in the vigor of my spirits, and had naturally a familiar moving voice, which is a great matter with the common hearers; and doing all in bodily weakness, as a dying man, my soul was the more easily brought to seriousness, and to preach as a dying man to dying men; for drowsy formality does but stupify the hearers and rock them asleep. It must be serious preaching which makes men serious in hearing and obeying it."

"Another advantage which I had was, the acceptation of my person. Though to win estimation and love to ourselves only, be an end that none but proud men and hypocrites intend, yet it is most certain that the acceptableness of the person ingratiates the message, and greatly prepares the people to receive the truth. Had they taken me to be ignorant, erroneous, scandalous, worldly, self-seeking, or such like, I could have expected small success among them.

"Another advantage which I had was through the zeal and diligence of the godly people of the place, who thirsted after the salvation of their neighbors, and were, in private, my assistants; and being dispersed through the town, they were ready, in almost all companies, to repress seducing words, and to justify godliness, and convince, reprove, and exhort men according to their needs; and also to teach them how to pray, and to help them to sanctify the Lord's day. Those people that had none in their families who could pray or repeat the sermons, went to the houses of their neighbors who could do it, and joined with them; so that some houses of the ablest men in each street were filled with them that could do nothing or little in their own.

"And the holy, humble, blameless lives of the religious was a great advantage to me. The malicious people could not say, Your professors here are as proud and covetous as any. But the blameless lives of godly people shamed opposers, and put to silence the ignorance of foolish men, and many were won by their good conversation."

"Our private meetings were a marvellous help to the propagating of godliness among them; for thereby truths that slipped away were recalled, and the seriousness of the people's minds renewed, and good desires cherished; and hereby their knowledge was much increased; and here the younger Christians learned to pray, by frequently hearing others. And here I had opportunity to know their case; for if any were touched and awakened in public, I would presently see them drop in to our private meetings."

"Another furtherance of my work was the works which I wrote and distributed among them. Of some small books I gave each family one, which came to about eight hundred; of the larger I gave fewer; and to every family that was poor, and had not a Bible, I gave a Bible. I had found, myself, the benefit of reading to be so great, that I could not but think it would be profitable to others.

"And it was a great advantage to me, that my neighbors were of such a trade as allowed them time enough to read or talk of holy things; for the town liveth upon the weaving of Kidderminster stuffs, and as they stand in their loom they can set a book before them, or edify one another."

"And I found that my single life afforded me much advantage; for I could the more easily take my people for my children, and think all that I had too little for them, in that I had no children of my own to tempt me to another way of using it. And being discharged from the most of family cares, keeping but one servant, I had the more time and liberty for the labors of my calling.

"And God made use of my practice of physic among them as a very great advantage to my ministry; for they that cared not for their souls, loved their lives and cared for their bodies. And by this they were made almost as observant as a tenant is of his landlord. Sometimes I could see before me in the church a very considerable part of the congregation, whose lives God had made me a means to save, or to recover their health; and doing it for nothing, so obliged them, that they would readily hear me.

"And it was a great advantage to me, that there were at last few that were bad, who had not some of their own relations converted. Many children were subjects of God's grace at fourteen, or fifteen or sixteen years of age; and this did marvellously reconcile the minds of their parents to godliness. They that would not hear me, would hear their own children. They that before could have talked against godliness, would not hear it spoken against when it was their children's case. Many that would not be brought to it themselves, were gratified that they had intelligent religious children. And we had some persons near eighty years of age, who are, I hope, in heaven, and the conversion of their own children was the chief means to overcome their prejudice, and old customs, and conceits.

"And God made great use of sickness to do good to many. For though sick-bed promises are usually soon forgotten, yet was it otherwise with many among us; and as soon as they were recovered, they first came to our private meetings, and so kept in a learning state, till further fruits of piety appeared."

"Another of my great advantages was, the true worth and unanimity of the honest ministers of the country round about us, who associated in a way of concord with us. Their preaching was powerful and sober; their spirits peaceable and meek, disowning the treasons and iniquities of the times, as well as we; they were wholly devoted to the winning of souls; self-denying, and of most blameless lives; evil spoken of by no sober men, but greatly beloved by their own people and all that knew them; adhering to no faction; neither Episcopal, Presbyterian, nor Independent, as to parties; but desiring union, and loving that which is good, in all."

"Another great help to my success at last, was the before described work of personal conference with every family apart, and catechising and instructing them. That which was spoken to them personally, and sometimes drew forth their answers, awakened their attention, and was more easily applied than public preaching, and seemed to do much more upon them.

"And the exercise of church discipline was no small furtherance of the people's good; for I found plainly, that without it I could not have kept the more spiritual from separations and divisions. There is something generally in their dispositions which inclines them to separate from open ungodly sinners, as men of another nature and society; and if they had not seen me do something reasonable for a regular separation of the notorious obstinate sinners from the rest, they would have withdrawn themselves irregularly; and it would not have been in my power to satisfy them."

"Another means of success was, directing my instructions to them in a suitableness to the main end, and yet so as might suit their dispositions and diseases. I daily opened to them, and with the greatest importunity labored to imprint upon their minds the great fundamental principles of Christianity, even a right knowledge and belief of, and subjection and love to God the Father, the Son, and the Holy Ghost; and love to all men, and concord with the church and one another. I daily so inculcated the knowledge of God our Creator, Redeemer and Sanctifier, and love and obedience to God, and unity with the spiritual church, and love to men and hope of life eternal, that these were the matter of their daily thoughts and discourses and indeed their religion. And yet I usually put something in my sermon which was above their own discovery, and which they had not known before; and this I did, that they might be kept humble, and still perceive their ignorance, and be willing to keep in a learning state. And I did this also to increase their knowledge and make religion pleasant to them, by a daily addition to their former light, and to draw them on with desire and delight. But these things which they did not know before, were not unprofitable controversies, which tended not to edification, nor novelties in doctrine, contrary to the universal church; but either such points as tended to illustrate the great doctrines before-mentioned, or usually about the right methodizing of them; as the opening of the true and profitable method of the creed or doctrine of faith, the Lord's prayer or matter of our desires, and the ten commandments or law of practice; which afford matter to add to the knowledge of most professors of religion a long time. And when that is done, they must be led on still further, by degrees, as they are capable; but so as not to leave the weak behind; and so as shall still be truly subservient to the great points of faith, hope, and love, holiness and unity, which must be still inculcated as the beginning and the end of all."

"And it much furthered my success, that I stayed still in this one place near two years before the wars, and above fourteen years after; for he that removeth often from place to place, may sow good seed in many places, but is not likely to see much fruit in any, unless some other skillful hand shall follow him to water it. It was a great advantage to me to have almost all the religious people of the place of my own instructing and informing; and that they were not formed into erroneous and factious principles before; and that I stayed to see them grown up to some confirmedness and maturity."

These passages strikingly depict the means and effects of a revival of religion. Only let love to the Redeemer burn with quenchless ardor in the breast, and eternity with its tremendous and unutterable consequences be distinctly realized; compassion to immortal spirits infuse its tenderness and solicitude throughout the soul; a deep and unfailing sense of ministerial responsibility rest upon the conscience; then all the powers, talents, and influence that can be commanded, will be brought into exercise, and made to bear with unceasing energy on the great work of saving immortal souls, and then the Lord will command his "blessing, even life for evermore."

The secret of Baxter's success, perhaps, consisted prominently in the zeal, affection, and perseverance he displayed in *following his people to their homes.* His visits from house to house were for the purpose of applying with more close and pungent force the truths which were taught from the pulpit, or learned in the systematic instructions which were given to families and to children. And it is remarkable that his success in the earliest period of his ministry was chiefly amongst the young. In the preface to his work entitled "Compassionate Counsel to all Young Men," &c. he observes—"At Kidderminster, where God most blessed my labors, my first and greatest success was with the youth: and what was a marvellous way of divine mercy, when God had touched the hearts of young people, and brought them to the love and obedience of the truth, the parents and grand-parents who had grown old in an ignorant and worldly state, embraced religion, led by the love of their children, whom they perceived to be made, by it, much wiser and better, and more dutiful to them."—"By much experience I have been made more sensible of the necessity of warning and instructing youth, than I was before. Many say reports have taught it to me; the sad complaints of mournful parents have taught it me; the sad observation of the willful impenitence of some of my acquaintance tells it me; the many scores, if not hundreds of bills, that have been publicly put up to me to pray for wicked and obstinate children, have told it me; and, by the grace of God, the penitent confessions, lamentations, and restitutions of many converts, have made me more particularly acquainted with their case; which moved me for a time, on my Thursday's lecture, the first of every month, to speak to youth and those that educate them."

The religious education of youth is of infinite importance to families and to a nation, to the church and the world.

The youthful members of his congregation should engage the anxious attention of every pastor. They are the hopes of his ministry. With them truth meets the readiest reception. Among them conversion most frequently takes place. From them the most valuable members of Christian society are obtained. Rising into life, their influence is exerted wholly on the side of truth and piety; and when more matured in years, their instructions and example benefit and bless their families, their connexions, and the world. The conversion of a soul in the period of youth prevents its entering on a course of sin, engages it to the practice of holiness, ensures the exertion of its influence in behalf of God and his cause through the whole of its earthly being; and thus a career of happiness begins which shall extend throughout eternity.

In connection with this statement of Baxter's labors and success, some notice may be taken of his work entitled the "Reformed Pastor," written expressly to arouse the attention and excite the efforts of the Christian ministry to the great work in which he himself had so successfully engaged. His reverend brethren had witnessed the astonishing results of his pastoral engagements, and were anxious to make some efforts to accomplish among their own people similar results. A day of fasting and prayer was appointed by themselves at Worcester, before entering on their untried labors, and Baxter was requested to preach on the occasion. He prepared his sermon, but his illness prevented his preaching. He therefore enlarged his sermon into a treatise, and published it. Concerning this work he says:

"I have very great cause to be thankful to God for the success of that book, as hoping many thousand souls are the better for it, in that it prevailed with many ministers to set upon that work which I there exhort them to. Even from beyond the seas I have had letters of request to direct them how they might promote that work, according as that book had convinced them that it was their duty. If God would but reform the ministry, and set them on their duties zealously and faithfully, the people would certainly be reformed. All churches either rise or fall as the ministry rise or fall, not in riches and worldly grandeur, but in knowledge, zeal, and ability for their work."

Many and just encomiums have been passed on this work. "In the whole compass of divinity there is scarcely any thing superior to it, in close pathetic appeals to the conscience of the minister of Christ, upon the primary duties of his office." The editor of a recent edition justly says, "Of the excellence of this work it is scarcely possible to speak in too high terms. For powerful, pathetic, pungent, and heart-piercing address, we know of no work on the pastoral care to be compared with it. Could we suppose it to be read by an angel, or by some other being possessed of an unfallen nature, the argumentation and expostulations of our author would be felt to be altogether irresistible: and hard must be the heart of that minister who can read it without being moved, melted, and overwhelmed: hard must be his heart, if he be not roused to greater faithfulness, diligence, and activity in winning souls to Christ. It is a work worthy of being printed in letters of gold. It deserves, at least, to be engraven on the heart of every minister. I cannot help suggesting to the friends of religion that they could not, perhaps, do more good at less expense, than by presenting copies of this work to the ministers of Christ throughout the country. They are the chief instruments through whom good is to be effected in any country. How important, then, must it be to stir them up to holy zeal and activity in the cause of the Redeemer! A tract given to a poor man may be the means of his conversion; but a work, such as this, presented to a minister, may, through his increased faithfulness and energy, prove the conversion of multitudes."

In addition to Baxter's numerous ministerial and pastoral labors, he was consulted by persons of all classes and professions on the various subjects connected with church and state, which at that period were hotly and fiercely agitated. His pacific disposition, and his desire to promote universal concord among all religious parties, were generally known. Hence his advice was eagerly sought by all. This must have occupied no small portion of his time, and caused him no little anxiety. He gives a curious account of his being consulted by Cromwell, and his preaching before him.

"At this time Lord Broghill and the Earl of Warwick brought me to preach before Cromwell, the protector, which was the only time that ever I preached to him, save once long before, when he was an inferior man among other auditors. I knew not which way to provoke him better to his duty, than by preaching on 1 Cor. 1 : 10, against the divisions and distractions of the church, and showing how mischievous a thing it was for politicans to maintain such divisions for their own ends, that they might fish in troubled waters, and keep the church, by its divisions, in a state of weakness, lest it should be able to offend them: and to show the necessity and means of union. But the plainness and nearness, I heard, was displeasing to him and his courtiers; yet they bore with it.

"A while after, Cromwell sent to speak with me; and when I came, in the presence only of three of his chief men, he began a long and tedious speech to me of God's providence in the change of the government, and how God had owned it, and what great things had been done at home and abroad, in the peace with Spain and Holland, &c. When he had wearied us all with speaking thus slowly about an hour, I told him it was too great condescension to acquaint me so fully with all these matters which were above me, but that we took our ancient monarchy to be a blessing, and not an evil to the land, and humbly craved his patience, that I might ask him how England had ever forfeited that blessing, and unto whom the forfeiture was made? I was led to speak of the species of government only, for they had lately made it treason by a law to speak for the person of the king. Upon that question he was awakened into some passion, and told me it was no forfeiture, but God had changed it as pleased him; and then he let fly at the parliament, which thwarted him; and especially by name at four or five of those members who were my chief acquaintance; and I presumed to defend them against his passion; and thus four or five hours were spent.

"A few days after, he sent for me again, to hear my judgment about liberty of conscience, which he pretended to be most zealous for, before almost all his privy council, where, after another slow, tedious speech of his, I told him a little of my judgment."

Baxter was also consulted by various private individuals on cases of conscience, which he was requested to solve. To these he lent a willing ear, and administered suitable advice; or he replied to them in suitable and interesting letters. This must have occupied his time considerably. Besides, during his residence at Kidderminster, and while pursuing his indefatigable labors among his flock, he wrote and published nearly *sixty different works*, many of them quarto volumes of considerable size. Among these may be specially enumerated, in addition to those already noticed, his "Call to the Unconverted,"* his "Treatise on Conversion," "On Self-denial," on "Crucifying the World," on "Peace of Conscience," &c. &c. &c.

These herculean labors seem incredible. But for the

* Published by the American Tract Society.

existence of the works themselves, his own declarations, and the concurring testimony of his several biographers, it would have been deemed impossible that, with his enfeebled health and incessant pain, he could have accomplished so much in so short a time.

His own account of his general labors shows at once his piety and devotedness, his spirit and energy, his zeal and perseverance. He remarks:

"But all these my labors, except my private conferences with the families, even preaching and preparing for it, were but my recreations, and, as it were, the work of my spare hours; for my writings were my chief daily labor, which yet went the more slowly on, that I never one hour had an amanuensis to dictate to, and especially because my weakness took up so much of my time. For all the pains that my infirmities ever brought upon me, were never half so grievous an affliction to me as the unavoidable loss of my time which they occasioned."

His treatise on "Self-denial" originated in his deep conviction of the "breadth, and length, and depth of the radical, universal, odious sin of selfishness." Under this conviction he preached a series of sermons on the subject, and, at the urgent entreaty of his friends, he published them in the form they now assume. He says that the work "found better acceptance than most of his others, but yet prevented not the ruin of church and state, and millions of souls by that sin."

Previous to this he had published his work on "Conversion." This he says "was taken from plain sermons which Mr. Baldwin had transcribed out of my notes. And though I had no leisure, in this or other writings, to take much care of the style, nor to add any ornaments, or citations of authors, I thought it might better pass as it was, than not at all; and that if the author missed of the applause of the learned, yet the book might be profitable to the ignorant, as it proved, through the great mercy of God."

Apologizing for the plainness and earnestness of his manner, he observes, "The commonness and the greatness of men's necessity commanded me to do any thing that I could for their relief, and to bring forth some water to cast upon this fire, though I had not at hand a silver vessel to carry it in, nor thought it the most fit. The plainest words are the most profitable oratory in the weightiest matters. Fineness is for ornament, and delicacy for delight; but they answer not necessity, though sometimes they may modestly attend that which answers it. Yea, when they are conjunct, it is hard for the necessitous hearer or reader to observe the matter of ornament and delicacy, and not to be carried from the matter of necessity; and to hear or read a neat, concise, sententious discourse, and not to be hurt by it; for it usually hinders the due operation of the matter, keeps it from the heart, stops it in the fancy and makes it seem as light as the style. We use not compliments when we run to quench a common fire, nor do we call men to escape from it by an eloquent speech. If we see a man fall into fire or water, we regard not the manner of plucking him out, but lay hands upon him as we can, without delay."

Baxter's "Call to the Unconverted" was made remarkably useful. He says, "The occasion of this was my converse with Bishop Usher, while I was at London, who, much approving my method or directions for peace of conscience, was importunate with me to write directions suited to the various states of Christians and also against particular sins. I reverenced the man, but disregarded these persuasions, supposing I could do nothing but what was done as well or better already. But when he was dead, his words went deeper to my mind, and I purposed to obey his counsel; yet so as that to the first sort of men, the ungodly, I thought vehement persuasions meeter than directions only. And so for such I published this little book, which God has blessed with unexpected success beyond all the rest that I have written, except the Saints' Rest. In a little more than a year there were about twenty thousand of them printed by my own consent, and about ten thousand since, besides many thousands by stolen impressions, which men stole for lucre's sake. Through God's mercy I have had information of almost whole households converted by this small book, which I set so light by. And as if all this in England, Scotland, and Ireland were not mercy enough to me, God, since I was silenced, has sent it over on his message to many beyond the seas; for when Mr. Eliot had printed the Bible in the Indian language, he next translated this my 'Call to the Unconverted,' as he wrote to us here."

In addition to its usefulness mentioned by Baxter himself, Dr. Bates relates an instance of six brothers being converted at one time by this invaluable book. To this work, multitudes now in glory, and many advancing thither, stand indebted for their first serious impressions. Urged by its awful denunciations, they have fled from the "city of destruction;" they have sought refuge at the cross of Calvary. Like the preaching of John, it awakens, alarms, and terrifies, that it may lead to peace, holiness, and glory, through Christ.

Among other methods of doing good, Baxter adopted the plan which is now so generally employed, of publishing small tracts, broadsheets, or handbills. He published various broadsheets, and had them affixed to walls and public buildings, that the attention of passengers might be arrested, and that those who had no leisure for larger works, or were indisposed to purchase treatises, might be informed, edified, and saved. This plan he adopted with great success during the raging of the plague.

This was certainly the most active, useful, and important period of his life. His labors subsequently to this were of a more chequered, desultory, and less obvious character. Their results, though undoubtedly great, inasmuch as he labored with the same zeal, piety, and devotedness as heretofore, yet could not be perceived so manifestly as when his efforts were concentrated in one spot, and were superintended by his untiring pastoral vigilance. The time of persecution for conscience' sake was at hand. He therefore, in common with multitudes of his brethren, was obliged to labor in such places, and on such occasions only, as the providence of God pointed out. But these labors were not in vain, for, as in days of old, they "that were scattered abroad, went every where preaching the word."

CHAPTER IV.

HIS ENGAGEMENTS AFTER LEAVING KIDDERMINSTER.

Baxter had acquired great celebrity, both as a preacher and writer. He was known, moreover, to be an ardent friend to civil and ecclesiastical peace. Hence he was frequently consulted on these subjects, not only by ministers, but by the higher powers. On various occasions he went to London, and it would seem chiefly on business relating both to the church and the nation. Early in April, 1660, he left Kidderminster, and reached London on the 13th of that month. The reason of his leaving is not stated, but it appears evidently to have been in connexion with the state of public affairs.

It was a saying of Baxter's, that we are "no more choosers of our employments than of our successes." The truth of this observation he was now especially called to verify by his own experience. On reaching London he was consulted on the subject of the (king's) "Restoration." This event he, in common with multitudes of his brethren, was desirous of seeing accomplished.

The new parliament appointed a day of fasting and prayer, and required Baxter to preach before them on the occasion. This occurred the day before the bill was passed for the return of the exiled monarch. Shortly after he was called to preach a thanksgiving sermon, on Monk's success, at St. Paul's, before the lord mayor and aldermen. Neither of the sermons appear to have given entire satisfaction. His moderate views displeased partizans of all sides: some charged him with sedition; others with vacillation and temporizing in politics. He was, however, a friend to the king, and rejoiced in the prospect of his restoration. He used all his efforts to promote its accomplishment.

When king Charles was restored, amid the general acclamations of the nation, several of the Presbyterian ministers were made chaplains in ordinary to him, among whom was Baxter. His certificate of appointment to the office is dated June 26, 1660. Various conferences were held by Baxter and his friends, to promote a union between episcopacy and presbyterianism. A meeting was held on the subject, in the presence of Charles, at which Baxter was the chief speaker. His address on the occasion is distinguished alike by its piety and fidelity. He was desirous of promoting and securing the religious liberties of the people, and of preventing those measures which he perceived were contemplated to remove many of the most holy and zealous preachers from their flocks. The following passage from his address to the king shows the efforts that had been made to preserve the Gospel ministry during the commonwealth, and his desire that, under the dominion of their rightful monarch, the same invaluable privilege might be preserved.

"I presumed to tell him (his majesty) that the people we spake for were such as were contented with an interest in heaven, and the liberty and advantages of the Gospel to promote it; and if this were taken from them, and they were deprived of their faithful pastors, and liberty of worshipping God, they would consider themselves undone in this world, whatever plenty else they should enjoy; and the hearts of his most faithful subjects, who hoped for his help, would even be broken; and that we doubted not but his majesty desired to govern a people made happy by him, and not a brokenhearted people, that considered themselves undone by the loss of that which is dearer to them than all the riches of the world. And I presumed to tell him that the late usurpers that were over us, so well understood their own interest, that, to promote it, they had found this way of doing good to be the most effectual means, and had placed and encouraged many thousand faithful ministers in the church, even such as detested their usurpation. And so far had they attained their ends hereby, that it was the principal means of their interest in the people, and the good opinion that any had conceived of them; and those of them that had taken the contrary course, had thereby broken themselves to pieces. Wherefore I humbly craved his majesty's patience that we might have the freedom to request of him that, as he was our lawful king, in whom all his people, save a few inconsiderable persons, were prepared to centre, as weary of their divisions, and glad of the satisfactory means of union in him, so he would be pleased to undertake this blessed work of promoting their holiness and concord; for it was not faction or disobedience which we desired him to indulge. And that he would never suffer himself to be tempted to undo the good which Cromwell or any other had done, because they were usurpers that did it; or discountenance a faithful ministry because his enemies had set them up. But that he would rather outgo them in doing good, and opposing and rejecting the ignorant and ungodly, of what opinion or party soever. For the people whose cause we recommended to him, had their eyes on him as the officer of God, to defend them in the possession of the helps of their salvation; which, if he were pleased to vouchsafe them, their estates and lives would be cheerfully offered to his service."

"The king gave us not only a free audience, but as gracious an answer as we could expect; professing his gladness to hear our inclinations to agreement, and his resolution to do his part to bring us together; and that it must not be by bringing one party over to the other, but by abating somewhat on both sides, and meeting in the midway; and that, if it were not accomplished, it should be of ourselves, and not of him: nay, that he was resolved to see it brought to pass, and that he would draw us together himself: with some more to this purpose. Insomuch that old Mr. Ash burst out into tears with joy, and could not forbear expressing what gladness this promise of his majesty had put into his heart."

Proposals of agreement were submitted to the king and his advisers, but without effect. Subsequently to this, Baxter was offered a bishopric by the lord chancellor; but this, for various reasons, he declined. He did not consider it "as a thing unlawful in itself," but he thought he "could better serve the church without it." In the letter in which he declines episcopal honors, he begs of the lord chancellor that he might be allowed to preach to his old charge at Kidderminster. He says:

"When I had refused a bishopric, I did it on such reasons as offended not the lord chancellor; and therefore, instead of it, I presumed to crave his favor to restore me to preach to my people at Kidderminster again, from whence I had been cast out, when many hundreds of others were ejected upon the restoration of all them that had been sequestered. It was but a vicarage; and the vicar was a poor, unlearned, ignorant, silly reader, that little understood what Christianity and the articles of his creed did signify; but once a quarter he said something which he called a sermon, which made him the pity or laughter of the people. This man, being unable to preach himself, kept always a curate under him to preach. Before the wars, I had preached there only as a lecturer, and he was bound in a bond of £500 to pay me £60 per annum, and afterwards he was sequestered, as is before sufficiently declared. My people were so dear to me, and I to them, that I would have been with them upon the lowest lawful terms. Some laughed at me for refusing a bishopric, and petitioning to be a reading vicar's curate. But I had little hopes of so good a condition, at least for any considerable time."

His application, however, proved unsuccessful; for arrangements could not be made between the patron and the chancellor respecting the removal of the old vicar, who retained the charge of four thousand souls, though utterly incompetent for his important duties, and Baxter was left without a charge.

Though not permitted to return to his charge, he nevertheless exerted himself in various ways to promote the glory of God and the good of souls. His attention was, at this period, drawn to the subject of missions among the North American Indians. Eliot, the "Apostle of the Indians," and his assistants, had effected much good among the roving tribes of America. Cromwell had entered warmly into the cause, and ordered collections to be made in every parish for the propagation of the Gospel in those regions. Funds were raised, a society was formed and incorporated, and much good was effected. At the "Restoration," some parties, inimical to the truth, endeavored to destroy the institution, and to appropriate the funds to other objects. Baxter, assisted by others, exerted himself to prevent this spoliation; and by his influence at court, succeeded in securing the property, and in restoring the society to its original design.

For his exertions he received a letter of thanks from the Governor of New England, and another from the venerable Eliot. The latter informs Baxter of his intention to translate the "Call to the Unconverted" into the Indian language, but waited for his permission, his counsel, and his prayers. To this letter Baxter replied. A few extracts from his reply will show the interest that both he and many others felt in the cause of missions in those troublous times.

"Reverend and much honored brother,—Though our sins have separated us from the people of our love and care, and deprived us of all public liberty of preaching the Gospel of our Lord, I greatly rejoice in the liberty, help and success which Christ has so long vouchsafed you in his work. There is no man on earth whose work I think more honorable than yours. To propagate the Gospel and kingdom of Christ in those dark parts of the world, is a better work than our hating and devouring one another. There are many here that would be ambitious of being your fellow-laborers, but that they are informed you have access to no greater a number of the Indians than you yourself and your present assistants are able to instruct. An honorable gentleman, Mr. Robert Boyle, the governor of the corporation for your work, a man of great learning and worth, and of a very public universal mind, did motion to me a public collection, in all our churches, for the maintaining of such ministers as are willing to go hence to you, while they are learning the Indian languages and laboring in the work, as also to transport them. But I find those backward that I have spoken to about it, partly suspecting it a design of those that would be rid of them; (but if it would promote the work of God, this objection were too carnal to be regarded by good men;) partly fearing that, when the money is gathered, the work may be frustrated by the alienation of it, but this I think they need not fear so far as to hinder any; partly because they think there will be nothing considerable gathered, because the people that are unwillingly divorced from their teachers will give nothing to send them farther from them, but specially because they think, on the aforesaid grounds, that there is no work for them to do if they were with you. There are many here, I conjecture, that would be glad to go any where, to Persians, Tartars, Indians, or any unbelieving nation, to propagate the Gospel, if they thought they could be serviceable; but the defect of their languages is their great discouragement. The industry of the jesuits and friars, and their successes in Congo, Japan, China, &c. shame us all, save you. I should be glad to learn from you how far your Indian tongue extends; how large or populous the country is that uses it, if it be known; and whether it reach only to a few scattered neighbors, who cannot themselves convey their knowledge far because of other languages. We very much rejoice in your happy work, the translation of the Bible, and bless God that hath strengthened you to finish it. If any thing of mine may be honored to contribute in the least measure to your blessed work, I shall have great cause to be thankful to God, and wholly submit the alteration and use of it to your wisdom."

The state of the heathen appears to have occupied the thoughts of Baxter through the whole course of his ministry. Numerous allusions and references to the subject are found in his writings. In the preface to his work entitled the "Reasons of the Christian Religion," he states that his desire to promote "the conversion of idolaters and infidels to God and the

Christian faith," was one of the reasons which prompted him to write that work. "The doleful thought that five parts of the world were still heathens and Mohammedans, and that Christian princes and preachers did no more for their recovery," awakened the most painful anxiety and distress in his mind. In his work, "How to do Good to Many," &c. he asks, "Is it not possible, at least, to help the poor ignorant Armenians, Greeks, Muscovites, and other Christians, who have no printing among them, nor much preaching and knowledge; and, for want of printing, have very few Bibles, even for their churches or ministers? Could nothing be done to get some Bibles, catechisms, and practical books printed in their own tongues, and given among them? I know there is difficulty in the way; but money, and willingness, and diligence, might do something. Might not something be done in other plantations, as well as in New-England, towards the conversion of the natives there? Might not some skillful, zealous preachers be sent thither, who would promote serious piety among those of the English that have too little of it, teach the natives the Gospel, and our planters how to behave themselves so as to win souls to Christ?"

How powerfully affecting, and yet how truly applicable, even at the present hour, is the following passage, contained in his life!—"It would make a believer's heart bleed, if any thing in the world will do it, to think that five parts in six of the world are still heathens, Mohammedans, and infidels, and that the wicked lives of Christians, with fopperies, ignorance, and divisions, form the great impediment to their conversion! to read and hear travelers and merchants tell that the Banians, and other heathens in Hindostan

Cambaia, and many other lands, and the Mohammedans adjoining to the Greeks, and the Abyssinians, &c. do commonly fly from Christianity, and say, 'God will not save us if we be Christians, for Christians are drunkards, and proud, and deceivers,' &c. and that the Mohammedans and many heathens have more, both of devotion and honesty, than nominal Christians that live among them! O wretched men, calling themselves after the name of Christ! that are not content to damn themselves, but thus lay stumbling-blocks before the world! It were better for these men that they had never been born!

At the close of his life, and on the near approach of eternity, his mind was deeply interested on this important subject. The unbounded benevolence of his heart is poured forth in the following extract from his solemn review of his own character, made in his last days:

"My soul is much more afflicted with the thoughts of the miserable world, and more drawn out in desire of their conversion, than heretofore. I was wont to look but little farther than England in my prayers, as not considering the state of the rest of the world: or, if I prayed for the conversion of the Jews, that was almost all. But now. as I better understand the case of the world, and the method of the Lord's prayer, so there is nothing that lies so heavy upon my heart as the thought of the miserable nations of the earth. It is the most astonishing part of all God's providence to me, that he so far forsakes almost all the world, and confines his special favor to so few; that so small a part of the world has the profession of Christianity, in comparison of heathens, Mohammedans, and infidels! and that, among professed Christians, there are so few that are saved from gross delusions, and have any competent knowledge; and that among those there are so few that are seriously religious, and truly set their hearts on heaven. I cannot be affected so much with the calamities of my own relations, or of the land of my nativity, as with the case of the heathen, Mohammedan, and ignorant nations of the earth. No part of my prayers is so deeply serious as that for the conversion of the infidel and ungodly world, that God's name may be sanctified, and his kingdom come, and his will be done on earth, as it is in heaven. Nor was I ever before so sensible what a plague the division of languages was, which hinders our speaking to them for their conversion; nor what a great sin tyranny is, which keeps out the Gospel from most of the nations of the world. Could we but go among Tartars, Turks, and heathens, and speak their language, I should be but little troubled for the silencing of eighteen hundred ministers at once in England, nor for all the rest that were cast out here, and in Scotland and Ireland. There being no employment in the world so desirable in my eyes, as to labor for the winning of such miserable souls, which makes me greatly honor Mr. John Eliot, the apostle of the Indians in New-England, and whoever else have labored in such work."

Baxter almost despaired of the conversion of the world. The obstacles to missionary enterprise were at that time insurmountable. "He that surveys the present state of the earth," writes Baxter to his friend Eliot, "and considers that scarcely a sixth part is Christian, and how small a part of them have much of the power of godliness, will be ready to think that Christ has called almost all his chosen, and is ready to forsake the earth, rather than that he intends us such blessed days as we desire." But "what hath God wrought!" How great the change in the state of religion, both at home and abroad, since the days of Baxter! Persecution has fled; religion has revived; the missionary spirit has been enkindled; prayer has been offered; money has been contributed; commerce has presented facilities for introducing the Gospel into all parts of the earth; wide and effectual doors have been opened; missionaries have gone forth to the help of the Lord against the mighty, and great success has attended their labors: so that we are evidently approaching nearer to the period when the proclamation shall be made, "The kingdoms of this world are become the kingdoms of our Lord, and of his Christ; and he shall reign for ever and ever."

About this period the celebrated "Savoy Conference" was held. The object was to effect a reconciliation between the different religious parties, that they might be united in one common profession of Christianity. At this conference Baxter took a prominent part. He was sincerely desirous for the peace of the church, and that an accommodation should ensue. For this purpose he submitted various propositions, but without effect: and, after some weeks' deliberation, the conference was broken up, without the least hope or possibility, under existing circumstances, of reconciliation. Baxter was charged by his antagonists with "speaking too boldly, and too long;" but this he accounted not a crime, but a virtue. "I thought it," says he, "a cause I could cheerfully suffer for; and should as willingly be a martyr for charity as for faith."

This was the last public and authorized attempt to promote peace and unity by argument and persuasion.

Thenceforward other measures were tried to effect so desirable an object, and, most unhappily, the divergence of the parties became greater than ever.

From the termination of the "Savoy Conference," the case of the dissidents became more trying and perplexing. They were calumniated and charged with preaching sedition, or with forming plots against the government. Baxter, whose loyalty was unimpeachable, and whose ruling passion was a desire for peace, whose very soul was love, appears to have been particularly marked as an object for the shafts of calumny. He says: "So vehement was the endeavor in court, city, and country, to make me contemptible and odious, as if the authors had thought that the safety either of church or state did lie upon it, and all would have been safe if I were but vilified and hated. So that any stranger that had but heard and seen all this, would have asked, What monster of villany is this man? and what is the wickedness that he is guilty of? Yet was I never questioned to this day before a magistrate. Nor do my adversaries charge me with any personal wrong to them; nor did they ever accuse me of any heresy, nor much contemn my judgment, nor ever accuse my life, but for preaching where another had been sequestered that was an insufficient reader, and for preaching to the soldiers of the parliament; though none of them knew my business there, nor the service that I did them. These are all the crimes, besides my writings, that I ever knew they charged my life with."

"Though no one accused me of any thing, nor spake a word to me of it, being (they knew I had long been) near a hundred miles off, yet did they defame me all over the land, as guilty of a plot; and when men were taken up and sent to prison, in other countries, it was said to be for Baxter's plot: so easy was it, and so necessary a thing it seemed then, to cast reproach upon my name."

During the two years of his residence in London, previous to his final ejectment, Baxter preached in various places, as opportunities presented themselves.

He says: "Being removed from my ancient flock in Worcestershire, and yet being uncertain whether I might return to them or not, I refused to take any other charge, but preached up and down London, for nothing, according as I was invited. When I had done thus above a year, I thought a fixed place was better, and so I joined with Dr. Bates, at St. Dunstan's in the West, in Fleet-street, and preached once a week, for which the people allowed me some maintenance. Before this time I scarcely ever preached a sermon in the city.

"The congregations being crowded, was that which provoked envy to accuse me; and one day the crowd drove me from my place. In the midst of a sermon at Dunstan's church, a little lime and dust, and perhaps a piece of a brick or two, fell down in the steeple or belfry, which alarmed the congregation with the idea that the steeple and church were falling; and indeed, in their confusion and haste to get away, the noise of the feet in the galleries sounded like the falling of the stones. I sat still in the pulpit, seeing and pitying their terror; and, as soon as I could be heard, I entreated their silence, and went on. The people were no sooner quieted, and got in again, and the auditory composed, but a wainscot bench, near the communion-table, broke with the weight of those who stood upon it; the noise renewed the fear, and they were worse disordered than before; so that one old woman was heard, at the church door, asking forgiveness of God for not taking the first warning, and promising, if God would deliver her this once, she would take heed of coming thither again. When they were again quieted I went on. But the church having before an ill name, as very old, and rotten, and dangerous, it was agreed to pull down all the roof and repair the building, which is now much more commodious.

"While these repairs were made I preached out my quarter at Bride's church, in the other end of Fleet-street; where the common prayer being used by the curate before sermon, I occasioned abundance to be at common prayer, who before avoided it. And yet accusations against me still continued.

"On the week days, Mr. Ashurst, with about twenty more citizens, desired me to preach a lecture in Milk-street, for which they allowed me forty pounds per annum, which I continued near a year, till we were all silenced. And at the same time I preached once every Lord's day at Blackfriars, where Mr. Gibbons, a judicious man, was minister. In Milk-street I took money, because it came not from the parishioners, but strangers, and so was no wrong to the minister, Mr. Vincent, a very holy, blameless man. But at Blackfriars I never took a penny, because it was the parishioners who called me, who would else be less able and ready to help their worthy pastor, who went to God by a consumption, a little after he was silenced. At these two churches I ended the course of my public ministry, unless God cause an undeserved resurrection."

"Shortly after our disputation at the Savoy, I went to Rickmansworth, in Hertfordshire, and preached there but once, upon Matt. 22 : 12, 'And he was speechless;' where I spake not a word that was any nearer kin to sedition, or that had any greater tendency to provoke them, than by showing 'that wicked men, and the refusers of grace, however they may now have many things to say to excuse their sins, will at last be speechless before God." Yet did the bishop of Worcester tell me, when he silenced me, that the bishop of London had showed him letters from one of the hearers, assuring him that I preached seditiously: so little security was any man's innocency to his reputation, if he had but one auditor that desired to get favor by accusing him.

"Shortly after my return to London I went into Worcestershire, to try whether it were possible to have any honest terms from the reading vicar there, that I might preach to my former flock; but when I had preached twice or thrice, he denied me liberty to preach any more. I offered him to take my lecture, which he was bound to allow me, under a bond of five hundred pounds, but he refused it. I next offered him to be his curate, and he refused it. I next offered him to preach for nothing, and he refused it. And lastly, I desired leave but once to administer the Lord's supper to the people, and preach my farewell sermon to them, but he would not consent. At last I understood that he was directed by his superiors to do what he did. But Mr. Baldwin, an able preacher whom I left there, was yet permitted.

"At that time, my aged father lying in great pain of the stone and strangury, I went to visit him, twenty miles further. And while I was there Mr. Baldwin came to me, and told me that he also was forbidden to preach. We both returned to Kidderminster."

"Having parted with my dear flock, I need not say with mutual tears, I left Mr Baldwin to live privately among them, and oversee them in my stead, and visit them from house to house; advising them, notwithstanding all the injuries they had received, and all the failings of the ministers that preached to them, and the defects of the present way of worship, that yet they should keep to the public assemblies, and make use of such helps as might be had in public, together with their private helps."

The great crisis, which was foreseen by many, had now arrived. The parliamentary attempt to promote ecclesiastical peace, by the "Act of Uniformity," demanding an oath of absolute subjection to every requisition of the church, ended in the ejectment of two thousand of the best and holiest ministers in the land from their livings and labors. Baxter determined on not taking the oath, and hence relinquished public preaching as soon as the act was passed, and before it came into operation. His reason for so doing, he states to be, that as his example was looked to by many throughout the country, it might be known that he could not conform.

In the earlier period of his ministry Baxter had resolved not to enter into the married state, that he might pursue his pastoral and ministerial labors with less anxiety and interruption. After his ejectment, however, having no public charge, and seeing little prospect of ever being able to resume his ministerial engagements, he deemed himself at liberty, and that it would conduce to his comfort, to be united in the bonds of matrimony. He married Miss Charlton, a lady who though much younger than himself, proved to be in every respect a suitable partner for this eminent saint.

His marriage excited much curiosity and remark throughout the kingdom; and "I think," he observes.

"the king's marriage was scarce more talked of than mine." He and his wife lived a very unsettled life; being obliged, on account of persecutions, frequently to remove from one place of residence to another.

He says: "Having lived three years and more in London since I left Kidderminster, but only three quarters of a year since my marriage, and finding it neither agree with my health or studies, the one being brought very low, and the other interrupted, and all public service being at an end, I betook myself to live in the country, at Acton, that I might set myself to writing, and do what service I could for posterity, and live, as much as possibly I could, out of the world. Thither I came, 1663, July 14, where I followed my studies privately in quietness, and went every Lord's day to the public assembly, when there was any preaching or catechising, and spent the rest of the day with my family, and a few poor neighbors that came in; spending now and then a day in London. And the next year, 1664, I had the company of divers godly faithful friends that tabled with me in summer, with whom I solaced myself with much content."

"On March 26, being the Lord's day, 1665, as I was preaching in a private house, where we received the Lord's supper, a bullet came in at the window among us, and passed by me, and narrowly missed the head of a sister-in-law of mine that was there, and hurt none of us; and we could never discover whence it came.

"In June following, an ancient gentlewoman, with her sons and daughter, came four miles in her coach, to hear me preach in my family, as out of special respect to me. It happened that, contrary to our custom, we let her knock long at the door, and did not open it; and so a second time, when she had gone away and came again; and the third time she came, we had ended. She was so earnest to know when she might come again to hear me, that I appointed her a time But before she came, I had secret intelligence, from one that was nigh her, that she came with a heart exceeding full of malice, resolving, if possible, to do me what mischief she could by accusation; and so that danger was avoided."

The "plague of London" now burst forth with tremendous fury, on which Baxter thus remarks:

"And now, after all the breaches on the churches, the ejection of the ministers, and impenitency under all, wars, and plague, and danger of famine began all at once on us. War with the Hollanders, which yet continues; and the driest winter, spring and summer that ever man alive knew, or our forefathers mention of late ages; so that the grounds were burnt, like the highways, where the cattle should have fed! The meadow grounds, where I lived, bare but four loads of hay, which before bare forty. The plague has seized on the most famous and most excellent city in Christendom, and at this time eight thousand die of all diseases in a week. It has scattered and consumed the inhabitants, multitudes being dead and fled. The calamities and cries of the diseased and impoverished are not to be conceived by those that are absent from them! Every man is a terror to his neighbor and himself; for God, for our sins, is a terror to us all. O! how is London, the place which God has honored with his Gospel above all the places of the earth, laid in low horrors, and wasted almost to desolation by the wrath of God, whom England hath contemned; and a God-hating generation are consumed in their sins, and the righteous are also taken away, as from greater evil yet to come."

"The number that died in London alone was about a hundred thousand. The richer sort removing out of the city, the greatest blow fell on the poor. At first, so few of the most religious were taken away, that, according to the mode of too many such, they began to be puffed up, and boast of the great difference which God made; but quickly after, they all fell alike. Yet not many pious ministers were taken away: I remember but three, who were all of my own acquaintance.

"It is scarcely possible for people that live in a time of health and security, to apprehend the dreadfulness of that pestilence! How fearful people were, thirty or forty, if not a hundred miles from London, of any thing that they bought from any mercer's or draper's shop! or of any goods that were brought to them! or of any person that came to their houses! How they would shut their doors against their friends! and if a man passed over the fields, how one would avoid another, as we did in the time of wars; and how every man was a terror to another! O how sinfully unthankful are we for our quiet societies, habitations, and health!"

Many of the ejected ministers seized the opportunity of preaching in the neglected or deserted pulpits, and in the public places of resort, to the terror-stricken inhabitants of London, and blessed results followed. "Those heard them one day often, that were sick the next, and quickly died. The face of death so awakened both preachers and hearers, that preachers exceeded themselves in fervent preaching, and the people crowded constantly to hear them; and all was done with such great seriousness that, through the blessing of

God, many were converted from their carelessness impenitency, and youthful lusts and vanities; and religion took such a hold on the people's hearts as could never afterwards be loosed."

When the plague reached Acton, in July, Mr. Baxter retired to Hampden, in Bucks, where he continued with his friend Mr. Hampden till the following March. The plague, he says, "having ceased on March 1st following, I returned home, and found the churchyard like a ploughed field with graves, and many of my neighbors dead; but my house, near the churchyard, uninfected, and that part of my family which I left there, all safe, through the great mercy of God."

Scarcely had the plague ceased its ravages before the great fire commenced its destructive career in London. Churches in great numbers were destroyed in the general conflagration. The zealous, though silenced watchmen, ventured, amid the ashes of a ruined city, to urge the inhabitants to flee from the "wrath to come," and to seek, in their impoverished condition, "the unsearchable riches of Christ."

The distress occasioned by these calamities was great. "Many thousands were cast into utter want and beggary, and many thousands of the formerly rich were disabled from relieving them." To the friends of Christ in London, the silenced ministers in the country had been accustomed to look for assistance in their distresses. By these providences their resources were in a measure dried up. But, though enduring dreadful privations, few, if any, were suffered to perish through want. Baxter says:

"Whilst I was living at Acton, as long as the act against conventicles was in force, though I preached to my family, few of the town came to hear me, partly because they thought it would endanger me, and partly for fear of suffering themselves, but especially because they were an ignorant poor people, and had no appetite for such things. But when the act was expired, there came so many that I wanted room; and when once they had come and heard, they afterwards came constantly; insomuch that in a little time there was a great number of them that seemed very seriously affected with the things they heard; and almost all the town, besides multitudes from Brentford and the neighboring places, came."

He attended the services of the church, and between the interval of service preached in his own house to as many as chose to come. This gave umbrage to the minister. "It pleased the parson," says Baxter, "that I came to church, and brought others with me; but he was not able to bear the sight of people's crowding into my house, though they heard him also; so that, though he spoke kindly to me, and we lived in seeming love and peace while he was there, yet he could not long endure it. And when I had brought the people to church to hear him, he would fall upon them with groundless reproaches, as if he had done it purposely to drive them away; and yet thought that my preaching to them, because it was in a private house, did all the mischief, though he never accused me of any thing that I spake. For I preached nothing but Christianity and submission to our superiors, faith, repentance, hope, love, humility, self-denial, meekness, patience, and obedience."

During his residence at Acton, Baxter became acquainted with Lord Chief Justice Hale, who occupied the house adjoining his own. With his simplicity, integrity, piety, and learning, he was delighted and charmed. He denominates him "the pillar of justice, the refuge of the subject who feared oppression, and one of the greatest honors of his majesty's government." His lordship, too, appears to have been equally interested in the character of his neighbor. His avowed esteem and respect for the despised nonconformist was a means of encouraging and strengthening the hands of Baxter. "When the people crowded in and out of my house to hear, he openly showed me such great respect before them at the door, and never spake a word against it, as was no small encouragement to the common people to go on; though the other sort muttered that a judge should seem so far to countenance that which they took to be against the law."

CHAPTER V.

HIS PERSECUTIONS, TRIAL, AND DEATH.

At length Baxter's preaching at Acton could no longer be connived at. Information was laid against him, and a warrant was issued for his apprehension. He was taken before two justices of the peace. "When I came," he writes, "they shut out all persons from the room, and would not give leave for any one person, no, not their own clerk or servant, or the constable, to hear a word that was said between us. Then they told me that I was convicted of keeping conventicles contrary to law, and so they would tender me the Oxford oath. I desired my accusers might come face to face, and that I might see and speak with the witnesses who testified that I kept conventicles contrary to the law, which I denied, as far as I understood law; but they would not grant it. I pressed that I might speak in the hearing of some witnesses, and not in secret; for I supposed that they were my judges, and that their presence and business made the place a place of judicature, where none should be excluded, or at least some should be admitted. But I could not prevail. Had I resolved on silence, they were resolved to proceed; and I thought a Christian should rather submit to violence, and give place to injuries, than stand upon his right, when it will give others occasion to account him obstinate. I asked them whether I might freely speak for myself, and they said yea; but, when I began to speak, still interrupted me, and put me by. But, with much importunity, I got them once to hear me, while I told them why I took not my meeting to be contrary to law, and why the Oxford act concerned me not, and they had no power to put that oath on me by the act; but all the answer I could get was, 'That they were satisfied of what they did.' And when, among other reasonings against their course, I told them, though Christ's ministers had, in many ages, been men esteemed and used as we now are, and their afflicters had insulted over them, the providence of God had still so ordered it that the names and memory of their silencers and afflicters have been left to posterity for a reproach, insomuch that I wondered that those who fear not God, and care not for their own or the people's souls, should yet be so careless of their fame, when honor seems so great a matter with them. To which Ross answered, that he desired no greater honor to his name, than that it should be remembered of him that he did this against me, and such as I, which he was doing."

The result of this interview was, that Baxter was fully committed, for six months, to the New Prison, Clerkenwell. He begged that his liberty might be granted till the following Monday; but as he would not promise not to preach on the intervening Lord's day, his request was denied.

The inhabitants of Acton were grieved at the loss of their neighbor, and the more so, as the incumbent of the parish was the means of his imprisonment. "The whole town of Acton were greatly exasperated against the dean when I was going to prison, insomuch that ever since they abhorred him as a selfish persecutor. Nor could he devise to do more to hinder the success of his (seldom) preaching there. But it was his own choice: 'Let them hate me, so they fear me.' And so I finally left that place, being grieved most that Satan had prevailed to stop the poor people in such hopeful beginnings of a common reformation, and that I was to be deprived of the exceeding grateful neighborhood of the Lord Chief Justice Hale, who could scarce refrain tears when he heard of the first warrant for my appearance.

"My imprisonment was, at present, no great suffering to me, for I had an honest jailer, who showed me all the kindness he could. I had a large room, and the liberty of walking in a fair garden; and my wife was never so cheerful a companion to me as in prison, and was very much against my seeking to be released; and she had brought so many necessaries, that we kept house as contentedly and as comfortably as at home, though in a narrower room; and I had the sight of more of my friends in a day, than I had at home in half a year."

Efforts were made, by his friends, to procure his release, which, in consequence of some informalities in his commitment, were successful. His reflections on his imprisonment show his piety and submission.

"While I stayed in prison, I saw somewhat to blame myself for, and somewhat to wonder at others for, and somewhat to advise my visitors about.

"I blamed myself that I was no more sensible of the spiritual part of my affliction; such as the interruption of my work among the poor people from whom I was removed, and the advantage Satan had got against them, and the loss of my own public liberty, for worshiping in the assemblies of God's people.

"I marvelled at some who suffered more than I, as Mr. Rutherford, when he was confined to Aberdeen, that their sufferings occasioned them such great joys as they express; which surely was from the free grace of God, to encourage others by their example, and not that their own impatience made them need it much more than at other times. For surely so small a suffering needs not a quarter of the patience which many poor nonconforming ministers, and thousands of others need, that are at liberty; whose own houses, through poverty, are made far worse to them than my prison was to me.

"I found reason to entreat my Acton neighbors not to let their passion against their parson, on my account, hinder them from a due regard to his doctrine, nor from any of the duty which they owed him; and to blame some who aggravated my sufferings, and to tell them that I had no mind to fancy myself hurt before I felt it. I used, at home to confine myself voluntarily almost as much. I had ten-fold more public life here, and converse with my friends, than I had at home. If I had been to take lodgings at London for six months, and had not known that this had been a prison, and had knocked at the door and asked for rooms, I should as soon have taken this which I was put into, as most in town, save only for the interruption of my sleep.

"I found cause to desire of my brethren, that, when they suffered, they would remember that the design of Satan was more against their souls than their bodies; that it was not the least of *his* hopes to destroy the love due to those by whom they suffered; to render our superiors odious to the people; and to make us take such a poor suffering as this for a sign of true grace, instead of faith, hope, love, mortification, and a heavenly mind; and that the loss of one grain of love was worse than a long imprisonment. Also that it much more concerned us to be sure that we deserve not suffering, than that we be delivered from it; and to see that we wrong not our superiors, than that they wrong not us; seeing we are not near so much hurt by their severities as we are by our sins. Some told me that they hoped this would make me stand a little further from the prelates and their worship than I had done. To whom I answered, that I wondered that they should think that a prison should change my judgment. I rather thought now it was my duty to set a stricter watch upon my passions, lest they should pervert my judgment, and carry me into extremes in opposition to those who afflicted me. If passion made me lose my love, or my religion, the loss would be my own. And truth did not change because I was in a jail."

His time was now chiefly occupied in writing and publishing various works on controversial and experimental divinity, and in making some attempts to procure a union between the Presbyterians and Independents. He frequently conversed and corresponded with Dr. Owen on this subject. Owen requested Baxter to draw up a scheme of agreement. This scheme Owen attentively considered, but could not adopt. Baxter's attempts to unite all parties satisfied none.

Baxter, with a few others of the nonconformists, defended the practice of occasional attendance and communion in the parish churches where the Gospel was preached. It was, in consequence, currently reported at this time, that he had actually conformed. He was offered preferment in Scotland by the king. A mitre, a professor's gown, or a surplice, was presented to his choice. But he declined accepting his majesty's offer. His refusal is contained in his letter to the Earl of Lauderdale, through whom the offer was presented.

"My Lord,—Being deeply sensible of your lordship's favors, and in special of your liberal offers for my entertainment in Scotland, I humbly return you my very hearty thanks. But these considerations forbid me to entertain any hopes or further thoughts of such a remove:

"1. The experience of my great weakness and decay of strength, and particularly of this last winter's pain, and how much worse I am in winter than in summer, doth fully persuade me that I should live but a little while in Scotland, and that in a disabled, useless condition, rather keeping my bed than the pulpit.

"2. I am engaged in writing a book, which, if I could hope to live to finish, is almost all the service that I expect to do God and his church more in the world—a Latin Metnodus Theologiæ; and I can hardly hope to live so long, it requiring near a year's labor more. Now, if I should go and spend that one half year, or year, which should finish that work, in travel, and the trouble of such a removal, and then leave my intended work undone, it would disappoint me of the ends of my life; for I live only for work, and therefore should remove only for work, and not for wealth and honor, if ever I remove.

"3. If I were there, all that I could hope for were liberty to preach the Gospel of salvation, and especially in some university among young scholars. But I hear that you have enough already for this work, that are like to do it better than I can.

"4. I have a family, and in it a mother-in-law, eighty years of age, of honorable extraction and great worth, whom I must not neglect, and who cannot travel. And it is to such a one as I, so great a business to remove a family, and all our goods and books so far, as deters me from thinking of it, having paid so dear for removals these eight years as I have done, and being but yesterday settled in a house which I have newly taken, and that with great trouble and loss of time.

"All this concurs to deprive me of this benefit of your lordship's favor. But, my lord, there are other fruits of it, which I am not altogether hopeless of receiving. When I am commanded to pray for kings, and all in authority, I am allowed the ambition of this preferment, which is all that ever I aspired after: 'to live a quiet and peaceable life, in all godliness and honesty.'

"I am weary of the noise of contentious revilers and have often had thoughts to go into a foreign land, if I could find any, where I might have a healthful air and quietness, that I might but live and die in peace. When I sit in a corner, and meddle with nobody, and hope the world will forget that I am alive, court, city, and country is still filled with clamors against me; and when a preacher wants preferment, his way is to preach or write a book against the nonconformists, and me by name. So that the press and pulpits of some, utter bloody invectives against myself, as if my peace were inconsistent with the kingdom's happiness. And never did my eyes read such impudent untruths, in matter of fact, as these writings contain; and they cry out for answers and reasons of my nonconformity, while they know the law forbids me to answer them unlicensed. I expect not that any favor or justice of my superiors should cure any of this. But a few things I would desire:

"1. If I might but be heard to speak for myself, before I be judged by them, and such things be believed. For to contemn the judgment of my rulers is to dishonor them.

"2. If I might live quietly to follow my private study, and might once again have the use of my books, which I have not seen these ten years, still paying for a room in which they stand at Kidderminster, where they are eaten with worms and rats, having no security for my quiet abode in any place long enough to encourage me to send for them. And if I might have the liberty that every beggar has, to travel from town to town; I mean, but to London, to oversee the press, when any thing of mine is licensed for it. And,

"3. If I be sent to Newgate for preaching Christ's Gospel, (for I dare not sacrilegiously renounce my calling, to which I am consecrated,) that I may have the favor of a better prison, where I may but walk and write.

"These I should take as very great favors, and acknowledge your lordship my benefactor, if you procure them. For I will not so much injure you as to desire, or my reason as to expect, any greater things, no, not the benefit of the law. I think I broke no law in any of the preachings which I am accused of; and I most confidently think that no law imposes on me the Oxford oath, any more than any conformable minister; and I am past doubting the present mittimus for my imprisonment is quite without law. But if the justices think otherwise now, or at any time, I know no remedy. I have yet a license to preach publicly in London diocess, under the archbishop's own hand and seal, which is yet valid for occasional sermons, though not for lectures or cures; but I dare not use it, because it is in the bishop's power to recall it. Would but the bishop, who, one would think, should not be against the preaching of the Gospel, not recall my license, I could preach occasional sermons, which would absolve my conscience from all obligations to private preaching. For it is not maintenance that I expect; I have never received a farthing for my preaching, to my knowledge, since May 1, 1662. I thank God I have food and raiment without being chargeable to any man, which is all that I desire, had I but leave to preach for nothing, and that only where there is a notorious necessity. I humbly crave your lordship's pardon for this tediousness, and again return you my very great thanks for your great favors; remaining, &c.

"*June* 24, 1670. RICHARD BAXTER."

He says: "On October 11, 1672, I fell into a dangerous fit of sickness, which God, in his wonted mercy, in time so far removed as to return me to some capacity of service.

"I had till now forborne, for several reasons, to seek a license for preaching from the king, upon the toleration. But when all others had taken theirs, and were settled in London and other places, as they could get opportunity, I delayed no longer, but sent to seek one on condition I might have it without the title of Independent, Presbyterian, or any other party, but only as a nonconformist. And before I sent, Sir Thomas Player, chamberlain of London, had procured it me without my knowledge or endeavor. I had sought none hitherto.

"1. Because I was unwilling to be, or seem any cause of that way of liberty, if a better might have been had, and therefore would not meddle in it.

"2. I lived ten miles from London, and thought it not just to come and set up a congregation there, till the ministers had fully settled theirs, who had borne the burden there in the times of the raging plague and fire, and other calamities, lest I should draw away any of their auditors, and hinder their maintenance.

"3. I perceived that no one, that ever I heard of till mine, could get a license, unless he would be entitled in it, a Presbyterian, Independent, or of some sect.

"The 19th of November was the first day, after ten years' silence, that I preached in a tolerated public assembly, though not yet tolerated in any consecrated church, but only, against law, in my own house.

"Some merchants set up a Tuesday's lecture in London, to be kept by six ministers at Pinner's Hall, allowing them twenty shillings a piece each sermon, of whom they chose me to be one."

"January 24, 1672-3, I began a Friday lecture at Mr. Turner's church in New-street, near Fetter-lane, with great convenience and God's encouraging blessing; but I never took a penny of money for it of any one. And on the Lord's days I had no congregation to preach to, but occasionally to any that desire me, being unwilling to set up a church and become the pastor of any, or take maintenance, in this distracted and unsettled way, unless further changes shall manifest it to be my duty. Nor did I ever yet administer the Lord's supper to any one person, but to my old flock at Kidderminster."

"On February 20th I took my house in Bloomsbury, in London, and removed thither with my family; God having mercifully given me three years' great peace among quiet neighbors at Totteridge, and much more health and ease than I expected, and some opportunity to serve him."

In this situation he continued for some time, employing his flying pen and his unwearied efforts to promote the peace of the churches and to instruct and bless mankind. In April, 1674, he writes, "God has so much increased my languishing, and laid me so low, that I have reason to think that my time on earth will not be long. And O how good has the will of God proved hitherto to me! And will it not be best at last? Experience causes me to say to his praise, 'Great peace have they that love his law, and nothing shall offend them; and though my flesh and heart fail, God is the rock of my heart and my portion for ever.

"At this time came out my book called 'The Poor Man's Family Book,' which the remembrance of the great use of Mr. Dent's 'Plain Man's Pathway to Heaven,' now laid by, occasioned me to write for poor country families, who cannot buy or read many books."

Anxiously bent on doing good, and encouraged by the reception and success his "Poor Man's Family Book" met with, he prepared several other works for the promotion and increase of family religion. He justly believed that domestic piety was of the utmost importance for the maintenance and progress of Christianity. To promote "household religion" he employed all his energies while at Kidderminster. In his "Reformed Pastor," he urges ministers seriously to consider the subject. He says: "The life of religion, and the welfare and glory, both of the church and state, depend much on family government and duty. If we suffer the neglect of this, we shall undo all. What are we like to do ourselves for reforming a congregation, if all the work be cast on us alone, and masters of families neglect that necessary duty of their own by which they are bound to help us? If any good be begun by the ministry in any soul, a careless, prayerless, worldly family, is likely to stifle it, or very much hinder it; whereas, if you could but get the rulers of families to do their duty, to take up the work where you left it, and help it on, what abundance of good might be done! I beseech you, therefore, if you desire the reformation and welfare of your people, do all you can to promote family religion."

He prosecuted his Master's work with unwearied zeal, though suffering great bodily affliction, and exposed to much vexatious and embarrassing opposition.

He says: "Taking it to be my duty to preach while toleration continues, I removed, the last spring, to London, where my diseases, increasing this winter, a constant head-ache added to the rest, and continuing strong for about half a year, constrained me to cease my Friday's lecture, and an afternoon sermon on the Lord's days in my house, to my grief; and to preach only one sermon a week, at St. James's market-house where some had hired an inconvenient place. But I had great encouragement to labor there, because of the notorious necessity of the people; it being the habitation of the most ignorant, atheistical, and popish about London; and because, beyond my expectation, the people generally proved exceedingly willing, and attentive, and tractable, and gave me great hopes of much success."

"On July 5, 1674, at our meeting over St. James's market-house, God vouchsafed us a great deliverance. A main beam, before weakened by the weight of the people, so cracked, that three times they ran in terror out of the room, thinking it was falling; but remembering the like at Dunstan's in the west, I reproved their fear as causeless. But the next day, taking up the boards, we found that two rents in the beam were so great that it was a wonder of Providence that the floor had not fallen, and the roof with it, to the destruction of multitudes. The Lord make us thankful!"

"It pleased God to give me marvellous encouragement in my preaching at St. James's. The crack having frightened away most of the richer sort, especially the women, most of the congregation were young men of the most capable age, who heard with great attention; and many that had not come to church for many years, manifested so great a change, (some papists, and divers others, returning public thanks to God for their conversion) as made all my charge and trouble easy to me. Among all the popish, rude, and ignorant people who were inhabitants of those parts, we had scarcely any that opened their mouths against us, and that did not speak well of the preaching of the word among them; though, when I came first thither, the most knowing inhabitants assured me that some of the same persons wished my death. Among the ruder sort, a common reformation was noticed in the place, in their conversation as well as in their judgments."

"The dangerous crack over the market-house at St. James's, made many desire that I had a larger safer place for meeting. And though my own dullness, and great backwardness to troublesome business, made me very averse to so great an undertaking, judging that, it being in the face of the court, it would never be endured, yet the great and incessant importunity of many, out of a fervent desire of the good of souls, constrained me to undertake it. And when it was almost finished, in Oxendon-street, Mr. Henry Coventry, one of his majesty's principal secretaries, who had a house joining to it, and was a member of parliament, spake twice against it in the parliament; but no one seconded him."

"And that we might do the more good, my wife urged the building of another meeting place in Bloomsbury, for Mr. Reed, to be furthered by my sometimes helping him; the neighborhood being very full of people, rich and poor.

"I was so long wearied with keeping my doors shut against them that came to distrain on my goods for preaching, that I was induced to go from my house, and to sell all my goods, and to hide my library first, and afterwards to sell it. So that if books had been my treasure, and I valued little more on earth, I had been now without a treasure. About twelve years I was driven a hundred miles from them; and when I had paid dear for the carriage, after two or three years I was forced to sell them. And the prelates, to hinder me from preaching, deprived me also of these private comforts. But God saw that they were my snare. We brought nothing into the world, and we must carry nothing out.

"I was the more willing to part with goods, books, and all, that I might have nothing to be distrained, and so go on to preach. And accordingly removing my dwelling to the new chapel which I had built, I purposed to venture there to preach, there being forty thousand persons in the parish, as is supposed, more than can hear in the parish church, who have no place to go to for God's public worship. So that I set not up church against church, but preached to those that must else have none, being unwilling that London should turn atheists, or live worse than infidels. But when I had preached there but once, a resolution was taken to surprise me the next day, and send me for six months to the common jail, upon the act for the Oxford oath. Not knowing of this, it being the hottest part of the year, I agreed to go for a few weeks into the country, twenty miles off. But the night before I should go, I fell so ill that I was induced to send to disappoint both the coach and my intended companion, Mr. Sylvester. And when I was thus fully resolved to stay, it pleased God, after the ordinary coach hour, that three men, from three parts of the city, met at my house accidentally, just at the same time, almost to a minute, of whom, if any one had not been there, I had not gone, namely, the coachman again to urge me, Mr. Sylvester, whom I had put off, and Dr. Coxe, who compelled me, and told me he would carry me into the coach. It proved a special merciful providence of

God; for after one week of languishing and pain, I had nine weeks greater ease than ever I expected in this world, and greater comfort in my work. My good friend Richard Berisford, Esq. clerk of the exchequer, whose importunity drew me to his house, spared no cost, labor, or kindness for my health or service."

Baxter was now constantly harassed with informations, fines, and warrants of distress, but he bore them all with astonishing meekness and patience. He endeavored to convince and convert the informers and officers, who, on several occasions, came to apprehend him. In some cases his exhortations were successful, if not to their actual conversion, at least to induce them to relinquish their persecuting practices.

A striking instance of his placable and forgiving disposition is given in the following extract. "Keting, the informer, being commonly detested for prosecuting me, was cast into jail for debt, and wrote to me to endeavor his deliverance, which I did; and in his letters says, 'Sir, I assure you I do verily believe that God has bestowed all this affliction on me because I was so vile a wretch as to trouble you. And I assure you I never did a thing in my life that has so much troubled myself as that did. I pray God to forgive me. And truly, I do not think of any that went that way to work, that ever God would favor with his mercy. And truly, without great mercy from God, I do not think that ever I shall thrive or prosper. And I hope you will be pleased to pray to God for me.'"

Baxter considered that the "vows of God were upon him," and that he must continue to preach wherever Divine providence opened a door for the purpose. His obligations to God he considered superior to those by which he was bound to obey the ordinances of man.

and therefore, though forbidden by law, and in despite of persecution, he continued to preach the Gospel to his ignorant and perishing countrymen.

He says: "Being driven from home, and having an old license of the bishop's yet in force, by the countenance of that, and the great industry of Mr. Berisford, I had leave and invitation for ten Lord's days to preach in the churches round about. The first that I preached in, after thirteen years' ejection and prohibition, was Rickmanworth, and after that, at Sarratt, at King's Langley, at Chesham, at Charlfont, and at Amersham, and that often twice a-day. Those heard who had not come to church for seven years; and two or three thousand heard, where scarcely a hundred were wont to come; and with so much attention and willingness, as gave me very great hopes that I never spake to them in vain. And thus soul and body had these special mercies."

"When I had been kept a whole year from preaching in the chapel which I built, on the 16th of April, 1676, I began in another, in a tempestuous time; such was the necessity of the parish of St. Martin's, where about 60,000 souls have no church to go to, nor any public worship of God! How long, Lord!"

"Being denied forcibly the use of the chapel which I had built, I was forced to let it stand empty, and pay thirty pounds per annum for the ground-rent myself, and glad to preach for nothing, near it, at a chapel built by another, formerly in Swallow-street, because it was among the same poor people that had no preaching."

Interruptions and informations were so numerous at Swallow-street that he was obliged to discontinue his labors there. "It pleased God to take away, by torment of the stone, that excellent faithful minister, Mr. Thomas Wadsworth, in Southwark; and just when I was thus kept out at Swallow-street, his flock invited me to Southwark, where, though I refused to be their pastor, I preached many months in peace, there being no justice willing to disturb us."

"When Dr. Lloyd became pastor of St Martin's in the Fields, I was encouraged by Dr. Tillotson to offer him my chapel in Oxendon-street for public worship, which he accepted, to my great satisfaction, and now there is constant preaching there. Be it by conformists or nonconformists, I rejoice that Christ is preached."

His reputation, too, was assailed. He was charged with uttering falsehood, and with the crime of murder! He was able, however, successfully to refute the calumnies, and to confound his calumniators.

About this period, 1681, Baxter was called to endure a severe and trying providence, in the death of his wife. They had lived together nineteen years. She had been his companion in tribulation; his comforter in sorrow. Animated by her piety and her influence, he had persevered in all his attempts to do good. But, now, in the advance of life, in weakened health, in persecution, and in no distant prospect of imprisonment, he was left to pursue his journey alone. She died in the faith and hope of the Gospel, June 17, 1681.

He still pursued his studies and his occasional labors. "Having been for retirement in the country, from July till August 14, 1682, returning in great weakness, I was able only to preach twice, of which the last was in my usual lecture in New-street, and it fell out to be August 24, just that day twenty years, that I, and near two thousand more, had been by law forbidden to preach any more. I was sensible of God's wonderful mercy that had kept so many of us twenty years in so much liberty and peace, while so many severe laws were in force against us, and so great a number were round about us who wanted neither malice nor power to afflict us. And so I took, that day, my leave of the pulpit and public work, in a thankful congregation. And it is likely indeed, to be my last.

"But after this, when I had ceased preaching, I was, being newly arisen from extremity of pain, suddenly surprised in my house by a poor violent informer, and many constables and officers, who rushed in and apprehended me, and served on me one warrant to seize on my person, for coming within five miles of a corporation; and five more warrants, to distrain for a hundred and ninety pounds for five sermons. They cast my servants into fears, and were about to take all my books and goods, and I contentedly went with them towards the justice to be sent to jail, and left my house to their will. But Dr. Thomas Coxe, meeting me, forced me in again to my couch and bed, and went to five justices and took his oath, without my knowledge, that I could not go to prison without danger of death. Upon that the justices delayed a day, till they could speak with the king, and told him what the doctor had sworn; and the king consented that the present imprisonment should be forborne, that I might die at home. But they executed all their warrants on my books and goods, even the bed that I lay sick on, and sold them all; and some friends paid them as much money as they were prized at, which I repaid."

"When I borrowed some necessaries I was never the quieter; for they threatened to come upon me again and take all as mine, whosesoever it was, which they found in my possession. So that I had no remedy, but utterly to forsake my house, and goods, and all, and take secret lodgings distant in a stranger's house. But having a long lease of my own house, which binds me to pay a greater rent than now it is worth, wherever I go I must pay that rent.

"The separation from my books would have been a greater part of my small affliction, but that I found I was near the end both of that work and life which needeth books, and so I easily let go all. Naked came I into the world, and naked must I go out.

"But I never wanted less what man can give, than when men had taken all. My old friends, and strangers to me, were so liberal, that I was constrained to check their bounty. Their kindness was a surer and larger revenue to me than my own.

"But God was pleased quickly to put me past all fear of man, and all desire of avoiding suffering from them by concealment, by laying on me more himself than man can do. Their imprisonment, with tolerable health, would have seemed a palace to me; and had they put me to death for such a duty as they persecute me for, it would have been a joyful end of my calamity. But day and night I groan and languish under God's just afflicting hand. As waves follow waves in the tempestuous seas, so one pain and danger follows another in this sinful miserable flesh. I die daily, and yet remain alive. God, in his great mercy, knowing my dullness in health and ease, makes it much easier to repent and hate my sin, and loath myself, and contemn the world, and submit to the sentence of death with willingness, than otherwise it was ever like to have been. O how little is it that wrathful enemies can do against us, in comparison of what our sin and the justice of God can do! And O how little is it that the best and kindest of friends can do for a pained body or a guilty soul, in comparison of one gracious look or word from God! Wo be to him that has no better help than man; and blessed is he whose help and hope is in the Lord."

"While I continued, night and day, under constant pain, and often strong, and under the sentence of approaching death by an incurable disease, which age and great debility yields to, I found great need of the constant exercise of patience by obedient submission to God; and, writing a small Tract of it for my own use, I saw reason to yield to them that desired it might be published, there being especially so common need of 'obedient patience.'"

"Under my daily pains I was drawn to a work which I had never the least thoughts of, and is like to be the last of my life, to write a paraphrase on the New Testament. Mr. John Humphrey having long importuned me to write a paraphrase on the Epistle to the Romans, when I had done that, the usefulness of it to myself drew me farther and farther, till I had done all. But having confessed my ignorance of the Revelation, and yet unwilling wholly to omit it, I gave but general notes, with the reasons of my uncertainty in the greatest difficulties, which I know will fall under the sharp censure of many. But truth is more valuable than such men's praises. I fitted the whole, by plainness, to the use of ordinary families.

"After many times deliverance from the sentence of death, on November 20, 1684, in the very entrance of the seventieth year of my age, God was pleased so greatly to increase my painful diseases, as to pass on me the sentence of a painful death. But God turns it to my good, and gives me a greater willingness to die than I once thought I should ever have attained. The Lord teach me more fully to love his will and rest therein, as much better than my own, that often strives against it.

"A little before this, while I lay in pain and languishing, the justices of sessions sent warrants to apprehend me, about a thousand more being also on the list, to be all bound to good behavior. I thought they would send me six months to prison for not taking the Oxford oath, and dwelling in London, and so I refused to open my chamber door to them, their warrant not being to break it open. But they set six officers at my study door, who watched all night, and kept me from my bed and food; so that the next day I yielded to them, who carried me, scarce able to stand, to their sessions, and bound me, in a four hundred pounds' bond, to good behavior. I desired to know what my crime was, and who were my accusers; but they told me it was for no fault, but to secure the government in evil times; and that they had a list of many suspected persons, who must do the like as well as I. I desired to know for what I was numbered with the suspected, and by whose accusation; but they gave me good words, and would not tell me. I told them I would rather they would send me to jail than put me in circumstances to wrong others by being bound with me in bonds that I was like to break to-morrow; for if there did but five persons come in when I was praying, they would take it for a breach of good behavior. They told me not, if they came on other business unexpectedly, and not to a set meeting; nor yet if we did nothing contrary to law, or the practice of the church. I told them our innocency was not now any security to us. If two beggar women did but stand in the street and swear that I spake contrary to the law, though they heard me not, my bonds and liberty were at their will; for I myself, lying on my bed, heard Mr. I. R. preach in a chapel on the other side of my chamber, and yet one Sibil Dash and Elizabeth Cappell swore to the justices that it was another that preached; two miserable poor women that made a trade of it, and had thus sworn against very many worthy persons in Hackney and elsewhere, on which their goods were seized for fines. But to all this I received no answer. I must give bond.

"But all this is so small a part of my suffering, in comparison of what I bear in my flesh, that I could scarce regard it; and it is small in comparison of what others suffer. Many excellent persons die in common jails: thousands are ruined. That holy humble man, Mr. Rosewell, is now under a verdict for death as a traitor for preaching some words, on the witness and oath of Hilton's wife, and one or two more women, whose husbands live professedly on the trade, for which he claims many hundred or thousand pounds. And not only the man declares, but many of his hearers witness, that no such words were spoken, nor any that did not become a loyal, prudent man.

"December 11, I was forced, in all my pain and weakness, to be carried to the sessions-house, or else my bond of four hundred pounds would have been judged forfeited. And the more moderate justices, that promised my discharge, would none of them be there, but left the work to Sir William Smith and the rest, who openly declared that they had nothing against me, and took me for innocent, but yet I must continue bound, lest others should expect to be discharged also, which I openly refused. But my sureties would be bound, lest I should die in jail, against my declared will, and so I must continue."

"January 17, I was forced again to be carried to the sessions, and after divers days good words, which put me in expectation of freedom, when I was gone, one justice, Sir ——— Deerham, said it was probable that these persons solicited for my liberty that they might come to hear me in conventicles; and on that they bound me again in a four hundred pounds' bond for above a quarter of a year, and so it is likely to be till I die, or worse; though no one ever accused me for any conventicle or preaching since they took all my books and goods above two years ago, and I, for the most part, keep my bed."

His greatest trial was now hastening. His "Paraphrase on the New Testament" gave great offence in certain quarters, and was made the ground of a trial for sedition.

The following account of this extraordinary trial and its issue are given by Calamy, and in a letter from a person who was present on the occasion:

"On the 28th of February Baxter was committed to the King's-Bench prison, by warrant of Lord Chief Justice Jefferies, for his 'Paraphrase on the New Testament,' which had been printed a little before, and which was described as a scandalous and seditious book against the government. On his commitment by the chief justice's warrant, he applied for a habeas corpus, and having obtained it, he absconded into the country to avoid imprisonment, till the term approached. He was induced to do this from the constant pain he endured, and an apprehension that he could not bear the confinement of a prison.

"On the 6th of May, which was the first day of the

term, he appeared in Westminster-Hall, and an information was then drawn up against him. On the 14th of May he pleaded not guilty to the information. On the 18th of the same month, being much indisposed, it was moved that he might have further time given him before his trial, but this was denied him. He moved for it by his counsel; but Jefferies cried out, in a passion, 'I will not give him a minute's time more, to save his life. We have had to do,' said he, 'with other sorts of persons, but now we have a saint to deal with; and I know how to deal with saints as well as sinners. Yonder,' said he, 'stands Oates in the pillory,' (as he actually did at that very time in the new Palace Yard,) 'and he says he suffers for the truth, and so says Baxter; but if Baxter did but stand on the other side of the pillory with him, I would say, two of the greatest rogues and rascals in the kingdom stood there.'

"On May 30, in the afternoon, Baxter was brought to trial before the lord chief justice at Guild-hall. Sir Henry Ashurst, who would not forsake his own and his father's friend, stood by him all the while. Baxter came first into court, and with all the marks of sincerity and composure, waited for the coming of the lord chief justice, who appeared quickly after, with great indignation in his face.

"'When I saw,' says an eye witness, 'the meek man stand before the flaming eyes and fierce looks of this bigot, I thought of Paul standing before Nero. The barbarous usage which he received drew plenty of tears from my eyes, as well as from others of the auditors and spectators.

"Jefferies no sooner sat down than a short cause was called and tried; after which the clerk began to read the title of another cause. 'You blockhead,' said

Jefferies, 'the next cause is between Richard Baxter and the king:' upon which Baxter's cause was called.

"On the jury being sworn, Baxter objected to them, as incompetent to his trial, owing to its peculiar nature. The jurymen being tradesmen, and not scholars, he alledged they were incapable of pronouncing whether his 'Paraphrase' was or was not according to the original text. He therefore prayed that he might have a jury of learned men, though the one-half of them should be papists. This objection, as might have been expected, was overruled by the court.

"The king's counsel opened the information at large, with its aggravations. Mr. Pollexfen, Mr. Wallop, Mr. Williams, Mr. Rotherham, Mr. Atwood, and Mr. Phipps, were Baxter's counsel, and had been engaged by Sir Henry Ashurst.

"Pollexfen then rose and addressed the court and the jury. He stated that he was counsel for the prisoner, and felt that he had a very unusual plea to manage. He had been obliged, he said, by the nature of the cause, to consult all our learned commentators, many of whom, learned, pious, and belonging to the church of England too, concurred with Mr. Baxter in his paraphrase of those passages of Scripture which were objected to in the indictment, and by whose help he would be enabled to manage his client's cause. 'I shall begin,' said he, 'with Dr. Hammond: and, gentlemen, though Mr. Baxter made an objection against you, as not fit judges of Greek, which has been overruled, I hope you understand English common sense, and can read.' To which the foreman of the jury made a profound bow, and said, 'Yes, sir.'

"On this the chief justice burst upon Pollexfen like a fury, and told him he should not sit there to hear him preach. 'No, my lord,' said Pollexfen, 'I am counsel for Mr. Baxter, and shall offer nothing but what is to the point.' 'Why, this is not,' said Jefferies, 'that you cant to the jury beforehand.' 'I beg your lordship's pardon,' said the counsel, 'and shall then proceed to business.' 'Come then,' said Jefferies, 'what do you say to this count? read it, clerk:' referring to the paraphrase on Mark, 12: 38–40. 'Is he not, now, an old knave, to interpret this as belonging to liturgies?' 'So do others,' replied Pollexfen, 'of the church of England, who would be loth so to wrong the cause of liturgies as to make them a novel invention, or not to be able to date them as early as the scribes and pharisees.' 'No, no, Mr. Pollexfen,' said the judge: 'they were long-winded, extempore prayers, such as they used to say when they appropriated God to themselves; "Lord, we are thy people, thy peculiar people, thy dear people."' And then he clenched his hands and lifted up his eyes, mimicking their manner, and running on furiously, as he said they used to pray. 'Pollexfen,' said Jefferies, 'this is an old rogue, who has poisoned the world with his Kidderminster doctrine. Don't we know how he preached formerly, "Curse ye Meroz; curse them bitterly that come not to the help of the Lord, to the help of the Lord against the mighty." He encouraged all the women and maids to bring their bodkins and thimbles to carry on their war against the king, of ever blessed memory. An old schismatical knave, a hypocritical villain!'

"Mr. Wallop said that he conceived the matter depending being a point of doctrine, it ought to be referred to the bishop, his ordinary: but if not, he humbly conceived the doctrine was innocent and justifiable, setting aside the inuendos, for which there was no color, there being no antecedent to refer them to, (*i. e.* no bishop or clergy of the church of England named;) he said the book accused contained many eternal truths: but they who drew the information were the libellers, in applying to the prelates of the church of England those severe things which were written concerning some prelates who deserved the characters which he gave. 'My lord,' said he, 'I humbly conceive the bishops Mr. Baxter speaks of, as your lordship, if you have read church history, must confess, were the plagues of the church and of the world.'

"Mr. Rotherham urged 'that if Mr. Baxter's book had sharp reflections upon the church of Rome by name, but spake well of the prelates of the church of England, it was to be presumed that the sharp reflections were intended only against the prelates of the church of Rome.' The lord chief justice said, 'Baxter was an enemy to the name and thing, the office and persons of bishops.' Rotherham added, that Baxter frequently attended divine service, went to the sacrament, and persuaded others to do so too, as was certainly and publicly known; and had, in the very book so charged, spoken very moderately and honorably of the bishops of the church of England.'

"Baxter added, 'My lord, I have been so moderate with respect to the church of England, that I have incurred the censure of many of the dissenters upon that account.' 'Baxter for bishops!' exclaimed Jefferies, 'that is a merry conceit indeed: turn to it, turn to it. Upon this Rotherham turned to a place where it is said 'that great respect is due to those truly called to be bishops among us; or to that purpose. 'Ay,' said Jefferies, 'this is your Presbyterian cant; *truly called to be bishops:* that is himself, and such rascals, called to be bishops of Kidderminster, and other such places. Bishops set apart by such factious Presbyterians as himself: a Kidderminster bishop he means.'

"Baxter beginning to speak again, Jefferies reviled him; 'Richard, Richard, dost thou think we'll hear thee poison the court? Richard, thou art an old fellow. an old knave; thou hast written books enough to load a cart, every one as full of sedition, I might say treason, as an egg is of meat. Hadst thou been whipped out of thy writing trade forty years ago, it had been happy. Thou pretendest to be a preacher of the Gospel of peace, and thou hast one foot in the grave: it is time for thee to begin to think what account thou intendest to give. But, leave thee to thyself, and I see thou'lt go on as thou hast begun; but, by the grace of God, I'll look after thee. I know thou hast a mighty party, and I see a great many of the brotherhood in corners, waiting to see what will become of their mighty don; and a doctor of the party (looking at Dr. Bates) at your elbow; but, by the grace of Almighty God, I'll crush you all. Come, what do you say for yourself, you old knave? come, speak up! What doth he say? I am not afraid of you, for all the snivelling calves you have about you:' alluding to some persons who were in tears about Mr. Baxter. 'Your lordship need not be,' said the holy man; 'for I'll not hurt you. But these things will surely be understood one day; what fools one sort of protestants are made to persecute the other!' And, lifting up his eyes to heaven, he said, 'I am not concerned to answer such stuff; but am ready to produce my writings for the confutation of all this; and my life and conversation are known to many in this nation.'

"Mr. Rotherham sitting down, Mr. Atwood began

to show that not one of the passages mentioned in the information ought to be strained to the sense which was put upon them by the inuendos; they being more natural when taken in a milder sense: nor could any one of them be applied to the prelates of the church of England, without a very forced construction. To rove this, he would have read some of the text: but Jefferies cried out, 'You shan't draw me into a conventicle with your annotations, nor your snivelling parson neither.' 'My lord,' said Mr. Atwood, 'that I may use the best authority, permit me to repeat your lordship's own words in that case.' 'No, you shan't,' said he: 'you need not speak, for you are an author already; though you speak and write impertinently.' Atwood replied, 'I can't help that, my lord, if my talent be no better; but it is my duty to do my best for my client.'

"Jefferies then went on inveighing against what Atwood had published; and Atwood justified it as in defence of the English constitution, declaring that he never disowned any thing that he had written. Jefferies several times ordered him to sit down; but he still went on. 'My lord,' said he, 'I have matter of law to urge for my client.' He then proceeded to cite several cases wherein it had been adjudged that words ought to be taken in the milder sense, and not to be strained by inuendos. 'Well,' said Jefferies, when he had done, 'you have had your say.'

"Mr. Williams and Mr. Phipps said nothing, for they saw it was to no purpose. At last Baxter himself said, 'My lord, I think I can clearly answer all that is laid to my charge, and I shall do it briefly. The sum is contained in these few papers, to which I shall add a little by testimony' But he would not hear a word.

At length the chief justice summed up the matter in a long and fulsome harangue. 'It was notoriously known,' he said, 'there had been a design to ruin the ki g and the nation. The old game had been renewed; and this person had been the main incendiary. He is as modest now as can be; but time was, when no man was so ready at, "Bind your kings in chains, and your nobles in fetters of iron;" and, "To your tents, O Israel." Gentlemen, (with an oath,) don't let us be gulled twice in an age.' And when he concluded, he told the jury 'that if they in their consciences believed he meant the bishops and clergy of the church of England in the passages which the information referred to, and he could mean nothing else, they must find him guilty. If not, they must find him not guilty.' When he had done, Baxter said to him, 'Does your lordship think any jury will pretend to pass a verdict upon me upon such a trial?' 'I'll warrant you, Mr. Baxter,' said he, 'don't you trouble yourself about that.'

"The jury immediately laid their heads together at the bar, and found him guilty. As he was going from the bar, Baxter told the lord chief justice, who had so loaded him with reproaches, and still continued them, that a predecessor of his had had other thoughts of him; upon which he replied, 'that there was not an honest man in England but what took him for a great knave.' Baxter had subpœnaed several clergymen, who appeared in court, but were of no use to him, through the violence of the chief justice. The trial being over, Sir Henry Ashurst led him through the crowd, and conveyed him away in his coach."

This is a faithful portrait of Jefferies, who furnished Bunyan with the features of his chief justice, the Lord Hategood. Can we be insensible to the mercies we enjoy in the very different administration of justice in our own times?

"On the 29th of June Baxter had judgment given against him. He was fined five hundred marks, condemned to lie in prison till he paid it, and bound to his good behavior for seven years. It is said that Jefferies proposed a corporal punishment, namely, whipping through the city; but his brethren would not accede to it. In consequence of which the fine and imprisonment were agreed to.

"Baxter being unable to pay the fine, and aware that, though he did, he might soon be prosecuted again, on some equally unjust pretence, went to prison. Here he was visited by his friends, and even by some of the respectable clergy of the church, who sympathised with his sufferings and deplored the injustice he received. He continued in this imprisonment nearly two years, during which he enjoyed more quietness than he had done for many years before.

"An imprisonment of two years would have been found very trying and irksome to most men; to Baxter, however, it does not appear to have proved so painful, though he had now lost his beloved wife, who had frequently before been his companion in solitude and suffering. His friends do not appear to have neglected or forgotten him. The following extract of a letter from the well known Matthew Henry, presents a pleasing view of the manner in which he endured bonds and afflictions for Christ's sake. It is addressed to his father, and dated the 17th of November, 1685, when Baxter had been several months confined. Mr. Williams justly remarks, 'It is one of those pictures of days which are past, which, if rightly viewed, may produce lasting and beneficial effects; emotions of sacred sorrow for the iniquity of persecution, and animating praise that the demon in these happy days of tranquillity is restrained, though not destroyed.'

" 'I went into Southwark, to Mr. Baxter. I was to wait upon him once before, and then he was busy. I found him in pretty comfortable circumstances, though a prisoner, in a private house near the prison, attended by his own man and maid. My good friend Mr. Samuel Lawrence went with me. He is in as good health as one can expect; and, methinks, looks better, and speaks heartier, than when I saw him last. The token you sent he would by no means be persuaded to accept (and was almost angry when I pressed it) from one ejected as well as himself. He said he did not use to receive; and I understand since, his need is not great.

" We sat with him about an hour. He gave us some good counsel to prepare for trials, and said the best preparation for them was a life of faith and a constant course of self-denial. He thought it harder constantly to deny temptations to sensual appetites and pleasures, than to resist one single temptation to deny Christ for fear of suffering; the former requiring such constant watchfulness; however, after the former, the latter will be the easier. He said, we who are young are apt to count upon great things, but we must not look for them; and much more to this purpose. He said he thought dying by sickness usually much more painful and dreadful than dying a violent death, especially considering the extraordinary supports which those have who suffer for righteousness' sake."

Various efforts were made by his friends to have his fine remitted, which, after considerable delay, was accomplished.

" On the 24th of November, 1686, Sir Samuel Astrey

sent his warrant to the keeper of the King's Bench prison to discharge Baxter. He gave sureties, however, for his good behavior, his majesty declaring, for his satisfaction, that it should not be interpreted a breach of good behavior for him to reside in London, which was not inconsistent with the Oxford act. After this release he continued to live some time within the rules of the Bench; till, on the 28th of February, 1687, he removed to his house in the Charterhouse-yard; and again, as far as his health would permit, assisted Mr. Sylvester in his public labors."

"After his injurious confinement," says his friend Sylvester, in the funeral sermon which he preached for Baxter, "he settled in Charterhouse-yard, in Rutlandhouse, and bestowed his ministerial assistance gratis upon me. Thereupon he attended every Lord's day in the morning, and every other Thursday morning at a weekly lecture. Thus were we yoked together in our ministerial work and trust, to our great mutual satisfaction; and because his respects to me, living and dying, were very great, I cannot but the more feel the loss. I had the benefit and pleasure of always free access to him, and instant conversation with him; and by whom could I profit more than by himself? So ready was he to communicate his thoughts to me, and so clearly would he represent them, as that I may truly say, it was greatly my own fault if he left me not wiser than he found me, at all times.

"After he had continued with me about four years and a half he was disabled from going forth to his ministerial work; so that what he did he performed for the residue of his life in his own hired house, where he opened his doors, morning and evening, every day, to all that would come to join in family worship with him; to whom he read the Holy Scriptures, from whence he 'preached the kingdom of God, and taught those things which concern the Lord Jesus Christ, with all confidence, no man forbidding him,' Acts, 28 : 30, 31, even as one greater than himself had done before him. But, alas, his growing diseases and infirmities soon forbade this also, confining him first to his chamber, and after to his bed. There, through pain and sickness, his body wasted; but his soul abode rational, strong in faith and hope, preserving itself in that patience, hope, and joy, through grace, which gave him great support, and kept out doubts and fears concerning his eternal welfare."

He still labored with his pen. Even on the very borders of eternity he was desirous to improve the fleeting moments. "He continued to preach," Dr. Bates observes, in his funeral discourse, "so long, notwithstanding his wasted, languishing body, that the last time he almost died in the pulpit. Not long after, he felt the approaches of death, and was confined to his sick-bed. Death reveals the secrets of the heart; then words are spoken with most feeling and least affectation. This excellent man was the same in his life and death; his last hours were spent in preparing others and himself to appear before God. He said to his friends that visited him, 'You come hither to learn to die; I am not the only person that must go this way. I can assure you that your whole life, be it ever so long, is little enough to prepare for death. Have a care of this vain, deceitful world, and the lusts of the flesh; be sure you choose God for your portion, heaven for your home, God's glory for your end, his word for your rule, and then you need never fear but we shall meet with comfort.'

"Never was penitent sinner more humble, never was a sincere believer more calm and comfortable. He acknowledged himself to be the vilest dunghill worm (it was his usual expression) that ever went to heaven. He admired the divine condescension to us, often saying, 'Lord, what is man; what am I, vile worm, to the great God!' Many times he prayed, 'God be merciful to me a sinner,' and blessed God that this was left upon record in the Gospel as an effectual prayer. He said, 'God may justly condemn me for the best duty I ever did; all my hopes are from the free mercy of God in Christ,' which he often prayed for.

"After a slumber, he waked, and said, 'I shall rest from my labor.' A minister then present said, 'And your works will follow you.' To whom he replied, 'No works; I will leave out works, if God will grant me the other.' When a friend was comforting him with the remembrance of the good many had received by his preaching and writings, he said, 'I was but a pen in God's hands, and what praise is due to a pen?'

"His resignation to the will of God in his sharp sickness was eminent. When extremity of pain constrained him earnestly to pray to God for his release by death, he would check himself: 'It is not fit for me to prescribe—when Thou wilt, what Thou wilt, how Thou wilt.'

"Being in great anguish, he said, 'O, how unsearchable are His ways, and his paths past finding out; the depths of his providence we cannot fathom!' And to his friends, 'Do not think the worse of religion for what you see me suffer.'

"Being often asked by his friends, how it was with his inward man, he replied, 'I bless God I have a well-grounded assurance of my eternal happiness, and great peace and comfort within.' But it was his regret that he could not triumphantly express it, by reason of his extreme pains. He said, 'Flesh must perish, and we must feel the perishing of it; and that though his judgment submitted, yet sense would still make him groan.'

"Being asked whether he had not great joy from his believing apprehensions of the invisible state, he replied, 'What else, think you, Christianity serves for?' He said, the consideration of the Deity in his glory and greatness was too high for our thought; but the consideration of the Son of God in our nature, and of the saints in heaven, whom he knew and loved, did much sweeten and familiarize heaven to him. The description of it, in Heb. 12:22–24, was most animating to him; 'that he was going to the innumerable company of angels, and to the general assembly and church of the first-born, whose names are written in heaven; and to God, the Judge of all, and to the spirits of just men made perfect, and to Jesus the Mediator of the new covenant, and to the blood of sprinkling that speaketh better things than the blood of Abel.' That scripture, he said, deserved a thousand thousand thoughts. O, how comfortable is that promise; 'Eye hath not seen, nor ear heard, neither have entered into the heart of man, the things which God hath prepared for them that love him.' At another time he said that he found great comfort and sweetness in repeating the words of the Lord's prayer, and was sorry some good people were prejudiced against the use of it, for there were all necessary petitions for soul and body contained in it. At other times he gave excellent counsel to young ministers that visited him; earnestly prayed God to bless their labors, and make them very successful in converting souls to Christ; expressed great joy in the hope that God would do a great deal of good by them; and that they were of moderate, peaceful spirits.

"He often prayed that God would be merciful to this miserable, distracted world; and that he would preserve his church and interest in it. He advised his friends to beware of self-conceit, as a sin that was likely to ruin this nation; and said, 'I have written a book against it, which I am afraid has done little good.' Being asked whether he had altered his mind on controversial points, he said, those that pleased might know his mind in his writings; and that what he had done was not for his own reputation, but for the glory of God.

"I went to him, with a very worthy friend, Mr. Mather, of New-England, the day before he died; and speaking some comforting words to him, he replied, 'I have pain; there is no arguing against sense; but I have peace, I have peace.' I said, you are now approaching your long-desired home; he answered, 'I believe, I believe.' He said to Mr. Mather, 'I bless God that you have accomplished your business; the Lord prolong your life.' He expressed his great willingness to die; and during his sickness, when the question was asked, 'How he did?' his reply was, 'Almost well.' His joy was most remarkable, when, in his own apprehension, death was nearest; and his spiritual joy was at length consummated in eternal joy."

"As to himself, even to the last," says Mr. Sylvester, "I never could perceive his peace and heavenly hopes assaulted or disturbed. I have often heard him greatly lament that he felt no greater liveliness in what appeared so great and clear to him, and so very much desired by him. As to the influence thereof upon his spirit, in order to the sensible refreshment of it, he clearly saw what ground he had to rejoice in God; he doubted not of his title to heaven, through the merits of Christ. He told me he knew it would be well with him when he was gone. He wondered to hear others speak of their so passionately strong desires to die, and of their transports of spirit when sensible of their approaching death, as he did not so vividly feel their strong consolations. But when I asked him whether much of this was not to be resolved into bodily constitution, he said it might be so. The heavenly state was the object of his severe and daily thoughts and solemn contemplations; for he set some time apart every day for that weighty work. He knew that neither grace nor duty could be duly exercised without serious meditation. And as he was a scribe instructed into the kingdom of heaven, so he both could and did draw forth out of his treasures things new and old, to his own satisfaction and advantage, as well as to the benefit of others."

"He had frequently, before his death, owned to me his continuance in the same sentiments that he had exhibited to the world in his polemic discourses, especially about justification, and the covenants of works and grace, &c. And being asked, at my request, whether he had changed his former thoughts about those things, his answer was, that he had told the world sufficiently his judgment concerning them by words and writing, and thither he referred men. And then lifting up his eyes to heaven, he uttered these words, 'Lord, pity, pity, pity the ignorance of this poor city.'

"On Monday, the day before his death, a great trembling and coldness awakened nature, and extorted strong cries for pity from Heaven; which cries and agony continued for some time, till at length he ceased those cries, and so lay in a patient expectation of his change. And being once asked by his faithful friend and constant attendant upon him in his weakness, worthy and faithful Mrs. Bushel, his housekeeper, whether he knew her or no, requesting some signification of it if he did, he softly said, 'Death, death!' And now he felt the benefit of his former preparations for such a trying hour. And, indeed, the last words that he spake to me, being informed that I was come to see him, were these, 'O, I thank him, I thank him;' and turning his eyes to me, he said, 'The Lord teach you to die.'"

"On Tuesday morning, about four o'clock, December 8th, 1691, he expired; though he expected and desired his dissolution to have been on the Lord's day before, which, with joy, to me he called a high day, because of his desired change expected then by him."

A report was quickly spread abroad after his death, that he was exercised on his dying bed with doubts respecting the truths of religion, and his own personal safety, which report Mr. Sylvester thus refutes:

"Of what absurdity will not degenerate man be guilty! We know nothing here that could, in the least, minister to such a report as this. I that was with him all along, have ever heard him triumphing in his heavenly expectation, and ever speaking like one that could never have thought it worth a man's while to be, were it not for the great interest and ends of godliness. He told me that he doubted not but it would be best for him, when he had left this life and was translated to the heavenly regions.

"He owned what he had written, with reference to the things of God, to the very last. He advised those that came near him, carefully to mind their soul's concerns. The shortness of time, the importance of eternity, the worth of souls, the greatness of God, the riches of the grace of Christ, the excellency and import of an heavenly mind and life, and the great usefulness of the word and means of grace pursuant to eternal purposes, ever lay pressingly upon his own heart, and extorted from him very useful directions and encouragements to all that came near him, even to the last; insomuch that if a polemical or casuistical point, or any speculation on philosophy or divinity, had been but offered to him for his resolution, after the clearest and briefest representation of his mind which the proposer's satisfaction called for, he presently and most delightfully fell into conversation about what related to our Christian hope and work."

"Baxter was buried in Christ-church, London, where the ashes of his wife and her mother had been deposited. His funeral was attended by a great number of persons of different ranks, especially of ministers, conformists as well as nonconformists, who were eager to testify their respect for one of whom it might have been said with equal truth, as of the intrepid reformer of the north, 'There lies the man who never feared the face of man.'"

In his last will, made two years before his death, he says, "I, Richard Baxter, of London, clerk, an unworthy servant of Jesus Christ, drawing to the end of this transitory life, having, through God's great mercy, the free use of my understanding, do make this my last will and testament, revoking all other wills formerly made by me. My spirit I commit, with trust and hope of the heavenly felicity, into the hands of Jesus, my glorified Redeemer and Intercessor; and, by his mediation, into the hands of God my reconciled Father, the infinite eternal Spirit, Light, Life and Love, most great, and wise, and good, the God of nature, grace and glory; of whom, and through whom, and to whom are all things; my absolute Owner, Ruler, Benefactor, whose I am, and whom I, though imperfectly, serve, seek and trust; to whom be glory for ever, amen. To him I render the most humble thanks, that he hath filled up my life with abundant mercy, and pardoned my sins by the merits of Christ, and vouchsafed, by his Spirit, to renew me and seal me as his own; and to moderate and bless to me my long sufferings in the flesh, and at last to sweeten them by his own interest and comforting approbation." He bequeathed his books to "poor scholars," and the residue of his property to the poor.

CHAPTER VI.

HIS PERSON—VIEWS OF HIMSELF, AND GENERAL CHARACTER.

Having proceeded to the grave, and committed his "remains to their long and final resting-place, it will be proper to present the views which were formed of his character, both by himself and friends.

"His person," Mr. Sylvester states, "was tall and slender, and stooped much; his countenance composed and grave, somewhat inclining to smile. He had a piercing eye, a very articulate speech, and his deportment rather plain than complimental. He had a great command over his thoughts. His character answered the description given of him by a learned man dissenting from him, after discourse with him; that 'he could say what he would, and he could prove what he said.'"

Some few years before his death, Baxter took a minute and extensive survey of his own character, and committed it to paper. From this paper the following extracts are taken:—

"As it is soul-experience which those that urge me to this kind of writing expect I should especially communicate to others, and I have said little of God's dealing with my soul since the time of my younger years, I shall only give the reader what is necessary to acquaint him truly what change God has made upon my mind and heart since those earlier times, and wherein I now differ in judgment and disposition from my former self. And, for any more particular account of heart-occurrences, and God's operations on me, I think it somewhat unsuitable to recite them; seeing God's dealings are much the same with all his servants in the main, and the points wherein he varieth are usually so small, that I think such not proper to be repeated. Nor have I any thing extraordinary to glory in, which is not common to the rest of my brethren, who have the same Spirit, and are servants of the same Lord. And the true reason why I do adventure so far upon the censure of the world as to tell them wherein the case is altered with me, is, that I may prevent young inexperienced Christians from being over-confident in their apprehensions, or overvaluing their first degrees of grace, or too much applauding and following unfurnished inexperienced men, and that they may be in some measure directed what mind and course of life to prefer, by the judgment of one that has tried both before them.

"The temper of my mind has somewhat altered with the temper of my body. When I was young, I was more vigorous, affectionate, and fervent in preaching, conference, and prayer, than ordinarily I can be now; my style was more extemporary and lax, but by the advantage of affection, and a very familiar moving voice and utterance, my preaching then did more affect the auditory than many of the last years before I gave over preaching; but yet what I delivered was much more raw, and had more passages that would not bear the trial of accurate judgments, and my discourses had both less substance and less judgment than of late.

"In my younger years my trouble for sin was most about my actual failings, in thought, word or action; now I am much more troubled for inward defects, and omission or want of the vital duties or graces in the soul. My daily trouble is so much for my ignorance of God, and weakness of belief, and want of greater love to God, and strangeness to him and to the life to come, and want of a greater willingness to die, and of a longing to be with God in heaven,—that I take not some immoralities, though very great, to be in themselves so great and odious sins, if they could be found separate from these. Had I all the riches of the world, how gladly should I give them for a fuller knowledge, belief, and love of God and everlasting glory! These wants are the greatest burdens of my life, which often make my life itself a burden. And I cannot find any hope of reaching so high in these while I am in the flesh, as I once hoped before this time to have attained; which makes me the more weary of this sinful world, which is honored with so little of the knowledge of God.

"Heretofore I placed much of my religion in tenderness of heart, and grieving for sin, and penitential tears; and less of it in the love of God, and studying his love and goodness, and in his joyful praises, than I now do. Then I was little sensible of the greatness and excellency of love and praise, though I coldly spake the same words in its commendation as I now do. And now I am less troubled for want of grief and tears, though I more value humility, and refuse not needful humiliation; but my conscience now looks at love and delight in God, and praising him, as the height of all my religious duties, for which it is that I value and use the rest.

"My judgment is much more for frequent and serious meditation on the heavenly blessedness, than it was in my younger days. I then thought that sermons on the attributes of God and the joys of heaven were not the most excellent; and was wont to say, 'Every body knows this, that God is great and good, and that heaven is a blessed place; I had rather hear how I may attain it.' And nothing pleased me so well as the doctrine of regeneration, and the marks of sincerity, because these subjects were suitable to me in that state; but now I had rather read, hear, or meditate on God and heaven, than on any other subject; for I perceive that it is the object that changes and elevates the mind, which will be like what it most frequently feeds upon; and that it is not only useful to our comfort to be much in heaven in our believing thoughts, but that it must animate all our other duties, and fortify us against every temptation and sin; and that a man is no more a Christian indeed, than as he is heavenly.

"I was once wont to meditate most on my own heart, and to dwell all at home, and look little higher. I was still poring either on my sins or wants, or examining my sincerity; but now, though I am greatly convinced of the need of heart-acquaintance and employment, yet I see more need of a higher work; and that I should look oftener upon Christ, and God, and heaven, than upon my own heart. At home I can find distempers to trouble me, and some evidences of my peace; but it is above that I must find matter of delight and joy, and love and peace itself. Therefore I would have one thought at home, upon myself and sins, and many thoughts above, upon the high, and amiable, and beatifying objects.

"Heretofore I knew much less than now, and yet was not half so much acquainted with my ignorance. I had a great delight in the daily new discoveries which I made, and in the light which shined upon me, like a man that comes into a country where he never was before; but I little knew either how imperfectly I understood those very points, whose discovery so much delighted me, nor how much might be said against them, nor how many things I was yet a stranger to; but now I find far greater darkness upon all things, and perceive how very little it is that we know in comparison of that which we are ignorant of, and I have far meaner thoughts of my own understanding, though I must needs know that it is better furnished than it was then.

"I now see more good and more evil in all men than heretofore I did. I see that good men are not so good as I once thought they were, but have more imperfections; and that nearer approach, and fuller trial, doth make the best appear more weak and faulty than their admirers at a distance think. And I find that few are so bad as either their malicious enemies or censorious separating professors do imagine.

"I less admire gifts of utterance and bare profession of religion than I once did; and have much more charity for many, who, by the want of gifts, do make an obscurer profession than they. I once thought that almost all that could pray movingly and fluently, and talk well of religion, were saints. But more observation has opened to me what odious crimes may consist with high profession; and I have met with divers obscure persons, not noted for any extraordinary profession or forwardness in religion, but only to live a quiet, blameless life, whom I have after found to have long lived, as far as I could discern, a truly godly and sanctified life; only their prayers and duties were, by accident, kept secret from other men's observation Yet he that, upon this pretence, would confound the godly and the ungodly, may as well go about to lay heaven and hell together.

"I am not so narrow in my special love as heretofore. Being less censorious, and talking more than I did for saints, it must needs follow that I love more as saints than I did before.

"I am much more sensible how prone many young professors are to spiritual pride and self-conceitedness and unruliness and division, and so to prove the grief of their teachers, and firebrands in the church; and how much of a minister's work lies in preventing this, and humbling and confirming such young inexperienced professors, and keeping them in order in their progress in religion.

"I am more deeply afflicted for the disagreements of Christians, than I was when I was a younger Christian. Except the case of the infidel world, nothing is so sad and grievous to my thoughts as the case of the divided churches; and therefore I am more deeply sensible of the sinfulness of those prelates and pastors of the churches who are the principal cause of these divisions. O how many millions of souls are kept by them in ignorance and ungodliness, and deluded by faction, as if it were true religion! How is the conversion of infidels hindered by them, and Christ and religion heinously dishonored!

"I am much less regardful of the approbation of man, and set much lighter by contempt or applause, than I did long ago. I am often suspicious that this is not only from the increase of self-denial and humility, but partly from my being glutted and surfeited with human applause; and all worldly things appear most vain and unsatisfactory when we have tried them most. But as far as I can perceive, the knowledge of man's nothingness, and God's transcendent greatness, with whom it is that I have most to do, and the sense of the brevity of human things, and the nearness of eternity, are the principal causes of this effect, which some have imputed to self-conceitedness and moroseness.

"I am more and more pleased with a solitary life; and though, in a way of self-denial, I could submit to the most public life, for the service of God, when he requires it, and would not be unprofitable that I might be private; yet, I must confess, it is much more pleasing to myself to be retired from the world, and to have very little to do with men, and to converse with God and conscience, and good books.

"Though I was never much tempted to the sin of covetousness, yet my fear of dying was wont to tell me that I was not sufficiently loosened from the world. But I find that it is comparatively very easy to me to be loose from this world, but hard to live by faith above. To despise earth is easy to me; but not so easy to be acquainted and conversant with heaven. I have nothing in this world which I could not easily let go; but, to get satisfying apprehensions of the other world is the great and grievous difficulty.

"I am much more apprehensive than long ago of the odiousness and danger of the sin of pride: scarce any sin appears more odious to me. Having daily more acquaintance with the lamentable naughtiness and frailty of man, and of the mischiefs of that sin, and especially in matters spiritual and ecclesiastical, I think, so far as any man is proud, he is kin to the devil, and a stranger to God and to himself. It is a wonder that it should be a possible sin, to men that still carry about with them, in soul and body, such humbling matter of remedy as we all do.

"I more than ever lament the unhappiness of the nobility, gentry, and great ones of the world, who live in such temptation to sensuality, curiosity, and wasting of their time about a multitude of little things; and whose lives are too often the transcript of the sins of Sodom—pride, fullness of bread, and abundance of idleness, and want of compassion to the poor. And I more value the life of the poor laboring man, but especially of him that hath neither poverty nor riches.

"I am much more sensible than heretofore, of the breadth, and length, and depth of the radical, universal, and odious sin of selfishness, and therefore have written so much against it; and of the excellency and necessity of self-denial, and of a public mind, and of loving our neighbor as ourselves.

"I am more and more sensible that most controversies have more need of right stating than of debating; and if my skill be increased in any thing, it is in narrowing controversies by explication, and separating the real from the verbal, and proving to many contenders that they in fact differ less than they think they do.

"I am more solicitous than I have been about my duty to God, and less solicitous about his dealings with me, as being assured that he will do all things well, acknowledging the goodness of all the declarations of his holiness, even in the punishment of man, and knowing that there is no rest but in the will and goodness of God.

"Though my habitual judgment, and resolution, and scope of life be still the same, yet I find a great mutability as to actual apprehensions and degrees of grace; and consequently find that so mutable a thing as the mind of man would never keep itself, if God were not its keeper.

"Thus much of the alterations of my soul, since my younger years, I thought best to give the reader, instead of all those experiences and actual motions and affections which I suppose him rather to have expected an account of. And having transcribed thus much of a life which God has read, and conscience has read, and must further read, I humbly lament it, and beg pardon of it, as sinful, and too unequal and unprofitable. And I warn the reader to amend that in his own, which he finds to have been amiss in mine; confessing, also, that much has been amiss which I have not here particularly mentioned, and that I have not lived according to the abundant mercies of the Lord But what I have recorded, has been especially to perform my vows, and to declare his praise to all generations, who has filled my days with his invaluable favors, and bound me to bless his name for ever.

"But having mentioned the changes which I think were for the better, I must add, that as I confessed many of my sins before, so, I have been since guilty of many, which, because materially they seemed small have had the less resistance, and yet, on the review, do trouble me more than if they had been greater, done in ignorance. It can be no small sin which is committed against knowledge, and conscience, and deliberation, whatever excuse it have. To have sinned whilst I preached and wrote against sin, and had such abundant and great obligations from God, and made so many promises against it, lays me very low; not so much in fear of hell, as in great displeasure against myself, and such self-abhorrence as would cause revenge against myself, were it not forbidden. When God forgives me, I cannot forgive myself; especially for any rash words or deeds, by which I have seemed injurious, and less tender and kind than I should have been to my near and dear relations, whose love abundantly obliged me; when such are dead, though we never differed in point of interest, or any great matter, every sour or cross provoking word which I gave them makes me almost irreconcileable to myself.

"I mention all these faults that they may be a warning to others to take heed, as they call on myself for repentance and watchfulness. O Lord, for the merits, and sacrifice, and intercession of Christ, be merciful to me a sinner, and forgive my known and unknown sins!"

Dr Bates has drawn a full-length portrait of the character of his venerable friend in his funeral sermon, from which some extracts will now be given.

"He had not the advantage of academical education; but, by the Divine blessing upon his rare dexterity and diligence, his eminence in sacred knowledge was such as few in the university ever arrive to."

"Conversion is the excellent work of Divine grace: the efficacy of the means is from the Supreme Mover. But God usually makes those ministers successful in that blessed work, whose principal design and delight is to glorify him in the saving of souls. This was the reigning affection in his heart; and he was extraordinarily qualified to obtain his end.

"His prayers were an effusion of the most lively melting expressions, growing out of his intimate ardent affections to God: from the abundance of his heart, his lips spake. His soul took wing for heaven, and wrapped up the souls of others with him. Never did I see or hear a holy minister address himself to God with more reverence and humility, with respect to his glorious greatness; never with more zeal and fervency, correspondent to the infinite moment of his requests; nor with more filial affiance in the Divine mercy."

As a specimen of his prayers, two quotations from his published writings may be given. Addressing the Divine Spirit, he says, "As thou art the Agent and Advocate of Jesus my Lord, O plead his cause effectually in my soul against the suggestions of Satan and my unbelief; and finish his healing, saving work, and let not the flesh or world prevail. Be in me the resident witness of my Lord, the Author of my prayers the Spirit of adoption, the seal of God, and the earnest of mine inheritance. Let not my nights be so long, and my days so short, nor sin eclipse those beams which have often illuminated my soul. Without these, books are senseless scrawls, studies are dreams, learning is a glow-worm, and wit is but wantonness, impertinence and folly. Transcribe those sacred precepts on my heart, which by thy dictates and inspirations are recorded in thy holy word. I refuse not thy help foi tears and groans; but O shed abroad that love upon my heart, which may keep it in a continual life of love. Teach me the work which I must do in heaven; refresh my soul with the delights of holiness, and the joys which arise from the believing hopes of the everlasting joys. Exercise my heart and tongue in the holy praises of my Lord. Strengthen me in sufferings; and conquer the terrors of death and hell. Make me the more heavenly, by how much the faster I am hastening to heaven; and let my last thoughts, words, and works on earth, be most like to those which shall be my first in the state of glorious immortality; where the kingdom is delivered up to the Father, and God will for ever be all, and in all; of whom, and through whom, and to whom, are all things, to whom be glory for ever. Amen."

Another specimen may be given from Baxter's conclusion of his work on the "Saints' Rest."

"O Thou, the merciful Father of spirits, the attractive of love, and ocean of delight! draw up these drossy hearts unto thyself, and keep them there till they are spiritualized and refined! Second thy servant's weak endeavors, and persuade those that read these lines to the practice of this delightful, heavenly work! O! suffer not the soul of thy most unworthy servant to be a stranger to those joys which he describes to others; but keep me, while I remain on earth, in daily breathing after thee, and in a believing, affectionate walking with thee. And, when thou comest, let me be found so doing; not serving my flesh, nor asleep with my lamp unfurnished, but waiting and longing for my Lord's return. Let those who shall read these pages, not merely read the fruit of my studies, but the breathing of my active hope and love; that if my heart were open to their view, they might there read thy love most deeply engraven with a beam from the face of the Son of God; and not find vanity, or lust, or pride within, where the words of life appear without; that so these lines may not witness against me; but proceeding from the heart of the writer, may they be effectual, through thy grace, upon the heart of the reader, and so be the savor of life to both."

Dr. Bates says: "In his sermons there was a rare union of arguments and motives to convince the mind and gain the heart. All the fountains of reason and persuasion were open to his discerning eye. There was no resisting the force of his discourses, without denying reason and Divine revelation. He had a marvellous felicity and copiousness in speaking. There was a noble negligence in his style; for his great mind could not stoop to the affected eloquence of words: he despised flashy oratory, but his expressions were clear and powerful; so convincing the understanding, so entering into the soul, so engaging the affections, that those were as deaf as adders who were not charmed by so wise a charmer. He was animated by the Holy Spirit, and breathed celestial fire, to inspire heat and life into dead sinners, and to melt the obdurate in their frozen tombs. Methinks I still hear him speak those powerful words: 'A wretch that is condemned to die to-morrow cannot forget it: and yet poor sinners, that continually are uncertain to live an hour, and certain speedily to see the majesty of the Lord, to their inconceivable joy or terror, as sure as they now live on earth, can forget these things, for which they have their memory; and which one would think, should drown the matters of this world, as the report of a cannon does a whisper, or as the sun obscures the poorest glow-worm. O wonderful stupidity of the unrenewed soul! O wonderful folly and madness of the ungodly! That ever men can forget—I say again, that they can forget eternal joy, eternal wo, and the eternal God, and the place of their eternal unchangeable abodes, when they stand even at the door; and there is but that thin veil of flesh between them and that amazing sight, that eternal gulf, and they are daily dying and stepping in."

To this may be added a quotation from a sermon preached before the judges at the assizes: "Honorable, worshipful, and well-beloved, it is a weighty employment that occasions your meeting here to-day. The estates and lives of men are in your hands. But it is another kind of judgment which you are all hastening towards; when judges and juries, the accusers and the accused, must all appear upon equal terms, for the final decision of a far greater cause. The case that is then and there to be determined, is not whether you shall have lands or no lands, life or no life, in our natural sense; but whether you shall have heaven or hell, salvation or damnation, and endless life of glory with God and the Redeemer, and the angels of heaven, or an endless life of torment with devils and ungodly men. As sure as you now sit on those seats, you shall shortly all appear before the Judge of all the world, and there receive an irreversible sentence to an unchangeable state of happiness or misery. This is the great business that should presently call up your most serious thoughts, and set all the powers of your souls on work for the most effectual preparation; that, if you are men, you may acquit yourselves like men, for the preventing of that dreadful doom which unprepared souls must there expect. The greatest of your secular affairs are but dreams and toys to this. Were you at every assize to determine causes of no lower value than the crowns and kingdoms of the monarchs of the earth, it were but as children's games to this. If any man of you believe not this, he is worse than the devil that tempteth him to unbelief; and let him know that unbelief is no prevention, nor will put off the day, or hinder his appearance; but will render certain his condemnation at that appearance.

"He that knows the law and the fact, may know before your assize what will become of every prisoner, if the proceedings be all just, as in our case they will certainly be. Christ will judge according to his laws; know, therefore, whom the law condemns or justifies, and you may know whom Christ will condemn or justify. And seeing all this is so, does it not concern us all to make a speedy trial of ourselves in preparation for this final trial? I shall, for your own sakes, therefore, take the boldness, as the officer of Christ, to summon you to appear before yourselves, and keep an assize this day in your own souls, and answer at the bar of conscience to what shall be charged upon you. Fear not the trial; for it is not conclusive, final, or a peremptory irreversible sentence that must now pass. Yet slight it not; for it is a necessary preparative to that which is final and irreversible."

After describing the vanities of the world, he bursts forth: "What! shall we prefer a mole-hill before a kingdom? A shadow before the substance? An hour before eternity? Nothing before all things? Vanity and vexation before felicity? The cross of Christ hath set up such a sun as quite darkeneth the light of worldly glory. Though earth were something, if there were no better to be had, it is nothing when heaven standeth by."

Dr. Bates further remarks: "Besides, his wonderful diligence in catechising the particular families under his charge was exceeding useful to plant religion in them. Personal instruction, and application of divine truths, has an excellent advantage and efficacy to insinuate and infuse religion into the minds and hearts of men, and, by the conversion of parents and masters to reform whole families that are under their immediate direction and government. His unwearied industry to do good to his flock, was answered by correspondent love and thankfulness. He was an angel in their esteem. He would often speak with great complacence of their dear affections; and, a little before his death, said, 'He believed they were more expressive of kindness to him, than the Christian converts were to the apostle Paul, by what appears in his writings.'"

"His books, for their number and the variety of matter in them, make a library. They contain a treasure of controversial, casuistical, positive, and practical divinity. Of them I shall relate the words of one whose exact judgment, joined with his moderation, will give a great value to his testimony; they are those of Dr Wilkins, afterwards bishop of Chester. He said tha Mr. Baxter had 'cultivated every subject he handled;'

and 'if he had lived in the primitive times, he had been one of the fathers of the church,' and 'that it was enough for one age to produce such a person as Mr. Baxter.' Indeed, he had such an amplitude in his thoughts, such a vivacity of imagination, and such solidity and depth of judgment as rarely meet in one man. His inquiring mind was freed from the servile dejection and bondage of an implicit faith. He adhered to the Scriptures as the perfect rule of faith, and searched whether the doctrines received and taught were consonant to it. This is the duty of every Christian according to his capacity, especially of ministers, and the necessary means to open the mind for Divine knowledge, and for the advancement of the truth."

"His books of practical divinity have been effectual for more numerous conversions of sinners to God than any printed in our time; and while the church remains on earth, will be of continual efficacy to recover lost souls. There is a vigorous pulse in them that keeps the reader awake and attentive. His book of the 'Saints' Everlasting Rest,' was written by him when languishing in the suspense of life and death, but has the signatures of his holy and vigorous mind. To allure our desires, he unveils the sanctuary above, and discovers the glory and joys of the blessed in the Divine presence, by a light so strong and lively, that all the glittering vanities of this world vanish in that comparison, and a sincere believer will despise them, as one of mature age does the toys and baubles of children. To excite our fear he removes the skreen, and makes the everlasting fire of hell so visible, and represents the tormenting passions of the damned in those dreadful colors, that, if duly considered, would check and control the unbridled licentious appetites of the most sensual."

Baxter's practical writings alone occupy four ponderous folio, or twenty-two octavo volumes. If a complete collection of his controversial and practical writings were made, they would occupy fully sixty volumes of the same size. "His industry was almost incredible in his studies. He had a sensitive nature, desirous of ease, as others have, and faculties like others, liable to tire; yet such was the continual application of himself to his great work, as if the labor of one day had supplied strength for another, and the willingness of the spirit had supported the weakness of the flesh." His painful and incessant afflictions would have prevented an ordinary man from attempting any thing; but he persevered with unwearied industry to the close of his days. His life was occupied, too, in active labors. In camps and at court, in his parish and in prison, at home and abroad, his efforts were unremitting and often successful.

Some idea of his sufferings may be formed from the summary of his diseases given by his late biographer.

"His constitution was naturally sound, but he was always very thin and weak, and early affected with nervous debility. At fourteen years of age he was seized with the small-pox, and soon after, by improper exposure to the cold, he was affected with a violent catarrh and cough. This continued for about two years, and was followed by spitting of blood and other phthisical symptoms. He became, from that time, the sport of medical treatment and experiment. One physician prescribed one mode of cure, and another a different one; till, from first to last, he had the advice of no less than thirty-six professors of the healing art. By their orders he took drugs without number, till, from experiencing how little they could do for him, he forsook them entirely, except some particular symptom urged him to seek present relief. He was diseased literally from head to foot; his stomach flatulent and acidulous; violent rheumatic head-aches; prodigious bleeding at the nose; his legs swelled and dropsical, &c His physicians called it hypochondria, he himself considered it *præmatura senectus*, premature old age; so that at twenty he had the symptoms, in addition to disease, of fourscore! To be more particular would be disagreeable; and to detail the innumerable remedies to which he was directed, or which he employed himself, would add little to the stock of medical knowledge. He was certainly one of the most diseased and afflicted men that ever reached the full ordinary limits of human life. How, in such circumstances, he was capable of the exertions he almost incessantly made, appears not a little mysterious. His behavior under them is a poignant reproof to many, who either sink entirely under common afflictions, or give way to indolence and trifling. For the acerbity of his temper we are now prepared with an ample apology. That he should have been occasionally fretful, and impatient of contradiction, is not surprising, considering the state of the earthen vessel in which his noble and active spirit was deposited. No man was more sensible of his obliquities of disposition than himself; and no man, perhaps, ever did more to maintain the ascendancy of Christian principle over the strength and waywardness of passion."

The conviction that his time would be short, urged him to prosecute his labors with unwearied assiduity. Love to immortal souls, too, exerted its powerful influence. This "love to the souls of men," says Dr Bates, "was the peculiar character of his spirit. In this he imitated and honored our Savior, who prayed, died, and lives for the salvation of souls. All his natural and supernatural endowments were subservient to that blessed end. It was his meat and drink, the life and joy of his life to do good to souls."

Disinterestedness formed no unimportant feature of his character, and was strikingly marked in his refusal of ecclesiastical preferment; his self-denying engagements respecting his stipend at Kidderminster; his gratuitous labors; abundant alms-giving; and the wide distribution of his works among the poor and destitute. So long as he had a bare maintenance he was content. He rejoiced in being able to benefit others by his property or his labors.

Fidelity to his Divine Master, and to his cause, was conspicuous in all his engagements. He tendered his advice, or administered his reproofs with equal faithfulness, whether in conrt or camp; to the king or to the protector; before parliament or his parishioners; in his conversation or his correspondence. He could not suffer sin upon his neighbor; and whatever he conceived would be for the benefit of those concerned, that he faithfully, and without compromise, administered. In his preaching he "shunned not to declare the whole counsel of God."

Dr. Bates remarks: "He that was so solicitous for the salvation of others, was not negligent of his own. In him the virtues of the contemplative and active life were eminently united. His time was spent in communion with God, and in charity to men. He lived above the world, and in solitude and silence conversed with God. The frequent and serious meditation of eternal things was the powerful means to make his heart holy and heavenly, and from thence his conversation. His life was a practical sermon, a drawing example. There was an air of humility and sanctity in his mortified countenance; and his deportment was becoming a stranger upon earth and a citizen of heaven."

The following passage from his interesting important work, entitled "The Divine Life," may be considered as a portrait of his own spiritual character.

"To walk with God," he says, "is a phrase so high, that I should have feared the guilt of arrogance in using it, if I had not found it in the Holy Scriptures. It is a phrase that imports so high and holy a frame of soul, and expresses such high and holy actions, that the naming of it strikes my heart with reverence, as if I had heard the voice to Moses, 'Put off thy shoes from off thy feet, for the place whereon thou standest is holy ground.' Methinks he that shall say to me, Come, see a man that walks with God, doth call me to see one that is next unto an angel or glorified soul. It is a far more reverend object in mine eye than ten thousand lords or princes, considered only in their earthly glory. It is a wiser action for people to run and crowd together to see a man that walks with God, than to see the pompous train of princes, their entertainments, or their triumph. O, happy man that walks with God, though neglected and contemned by all about him! What blessed sights does he daily see! What ravishing tidings, what pleasant melody does he daily hear! What delectable food does he daily taste! He sees, by faith, the God, the glory which the blessed spirits see at hand by nearest intuition! He sees that in a glass, and darkly, which they behold with open face! He sees the glorious majesty of his Creator, the eternal King, the Cause of causes, the Composer, Upholder, Preserver, and Governor of all worlds! He beholds the wonderful methods of his providence; and what he cannot fully see he admires, and waits for the time when that also shall be open to his view! He sees, by faith, the world of spirits, the hosts that attend the throne of God; their perfect righteousness, their full devotedness to God; their ardent love, their flaming zeal, their ready and cheerful obedience, their dignity and shining glory, in which the lowest of them exceed that which the disciples saw on Moses and Elias, when they appeared on the holy mount and talked with Christ! He hears by faith the heavenly concert, the high and harmonious songs of praise, the joyful triumphs of crowned saints, the sweet commemorations of the things that were done and suffered on earth, with the praises of Him that redeemed them by his blood, and made them kings and priests unto God. Herein he has sometimes a sweet foretaste of the everlasting pleasures which, though it be but little, as Jonathan's honey on the end of his rod, or as the clusters brought from Canaan into the wilderness; yet is more excellent than all the delights of sinners."

His character may be summed up in the words of Mr. Orme: "Among his contemporaries there were men of equal talents, of more amiable dispositions, and of greater learning. But there was no man in whom there appears to have been so little of earth, and so much of heaven; so small a portion of the alloy of humanity, and so large a portion of all that is celestial. He felt scarcely any of the attractions of this world, but felt and manifested the most powerful affinity for the world to come."

END.

www.ingramcontent.com/pod-product-compliance
Lightning Source LLC
LaVergne TN
LVHW021412110826
845150LV00007B/1894

* 9 7 8 1 4 2 5 5 1 1 0 7 4 *